Welcome to "Cross Stitch P Christmas Quotes"

This book features 65 festive Christmas quote cross-stitch patterns, thoughtfully designed for stitchers of all levels.

Perfect for quick projects and creative gifting, these patterns are ideal for framing, decorating, or adding a handmade touch to your holiday season. Get ready to stitch your way into the Christmas spirit—one quote at a time!

Happy stitching!

TIPS for a perfect stitching experience:
- Start at the center of the pattern for better alignment.
- Use an embroidery hoop to maintain even tension.

Share your finished project on Instagram! Tag **@alemixstitch**
I'd love to see your work!

HO HO HO POUR THE MERLOT
DEAR Santa I REALLY TRIED
DEAR SANTA IT'S A LONG STORY
Christmas Baking CREW
I SLEIGH
MILK AND cookies FOR SANTA
Christmas LOADING
RUDOLPh IS MY bestie
SANTA STOP HERE
CHRISTMAS calories DON'T COUNT
Believe IN SANTA
MAY JOY FILL YOUR HOME AND PEACE FIND IT'S WAY TO YOU THIS SEASON
holiday baking TEAM
I just want TO WATCH Christmas MOVIES
WHAT THE ELF?
DEAR Santa IT WAS THE DOG
Dear SANTA, IT WAS THE Cat

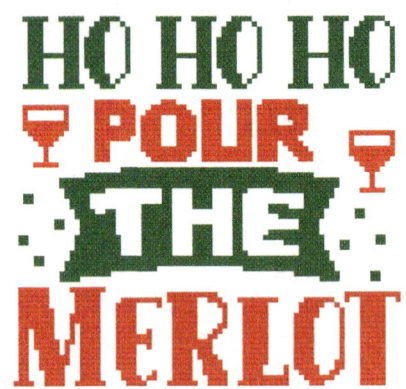

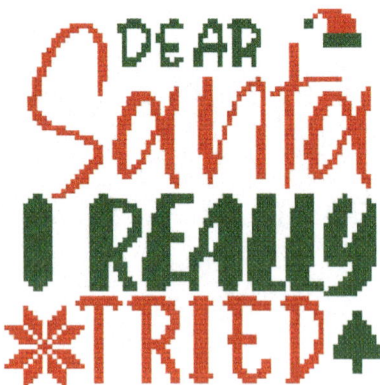

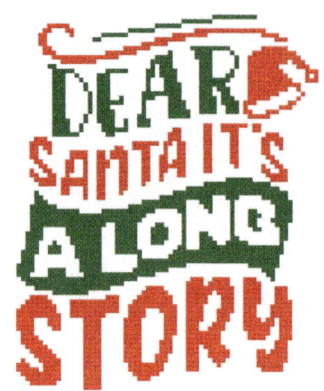

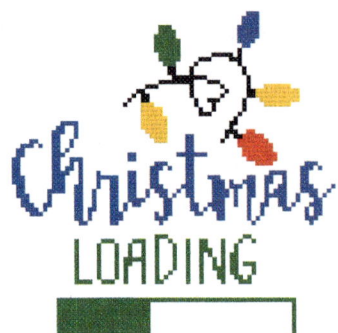

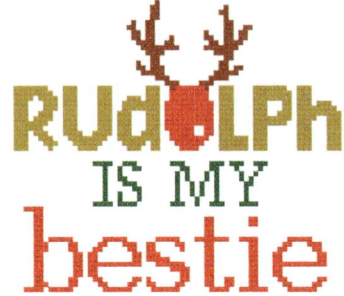

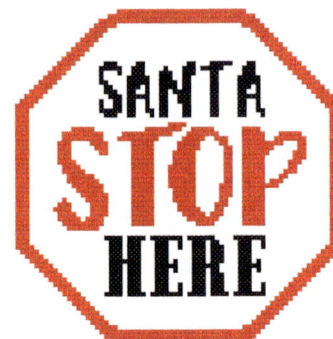

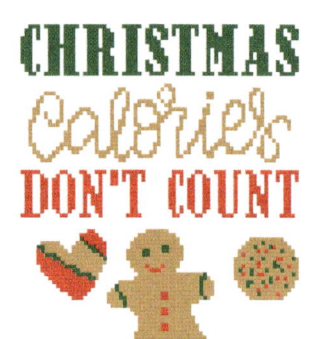

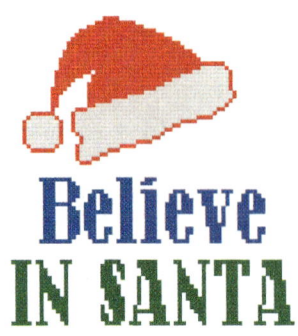

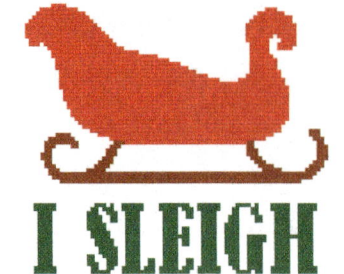

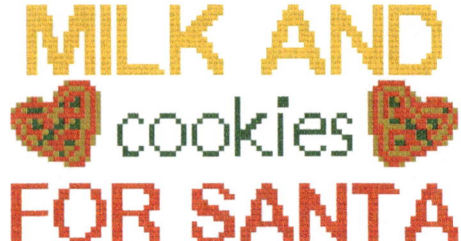

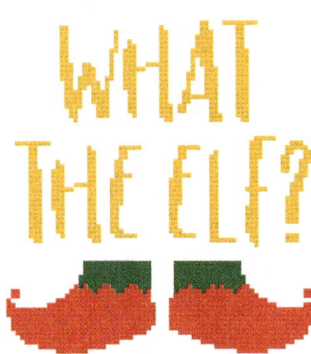

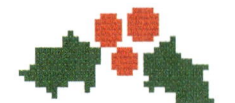

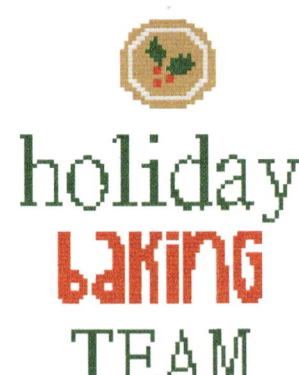

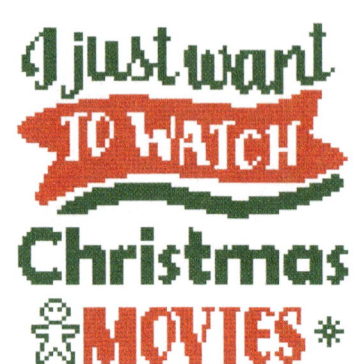

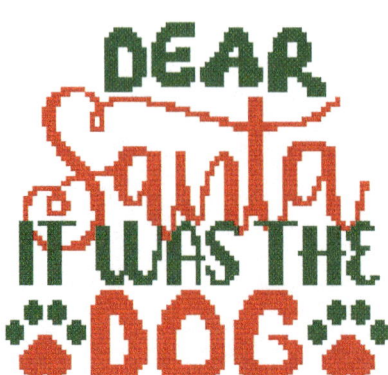

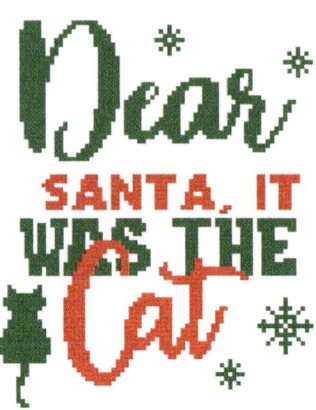

Dear Santa I'VE BEEN GOOD
DABBING THROUGH THE SNOW
BELIEVE IN THE MAGIC OF Christmas
DEAR SANTA IT WAS Framed
WILL TRADE BROTHER FOR Presents
Dear SANTA, will trade SISTER for PRESENTS
NICE WITH A HINT OF NAUGHTY
DEAR SANTA IT WAS JUST A Phase
IT'S Christmas TIME
CHRISTMAS vibes
MERRY MERRY MERRY CHRISTMAS
We wish you a Merry Christmas
There is no place like HOME for the holidays
Merry Christmas
What up GRINCHES
Proud MEMBER of the NAUGHTY list
BE MERRY Y'ALL

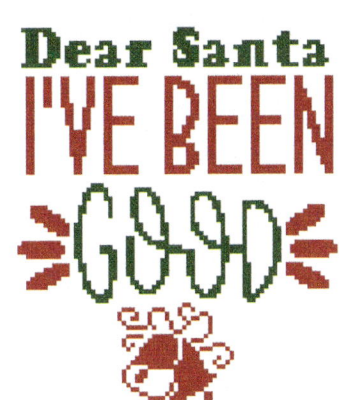

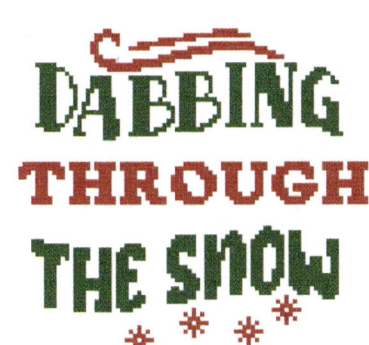

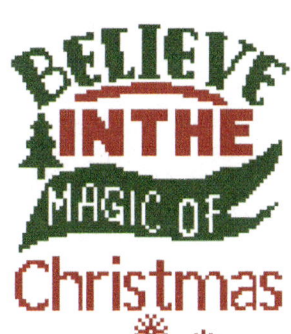

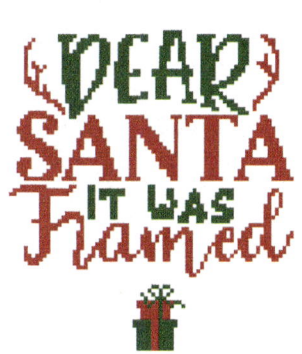

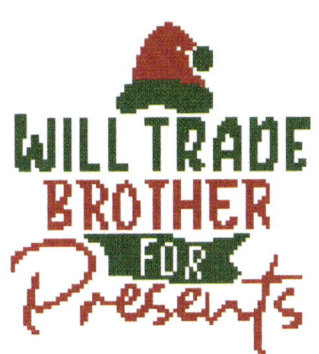

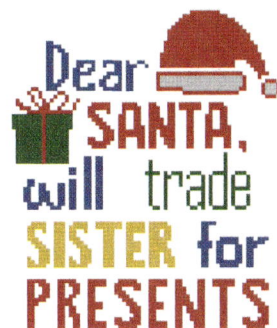

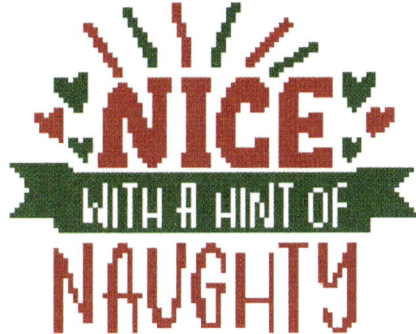

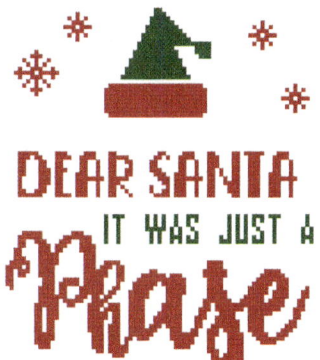

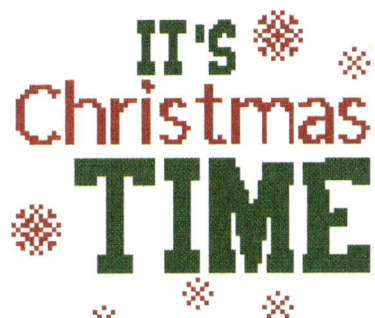

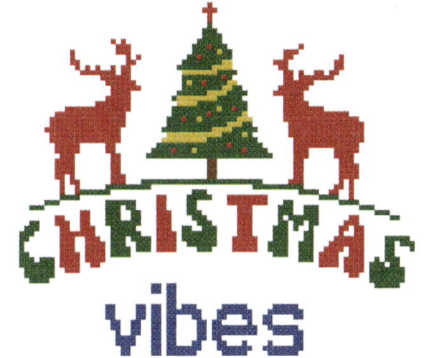

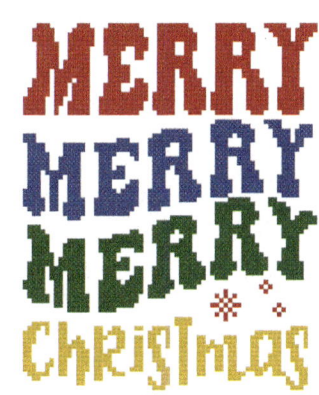

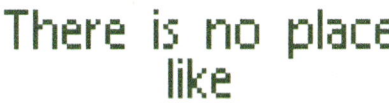

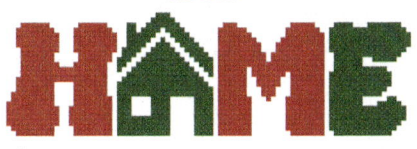

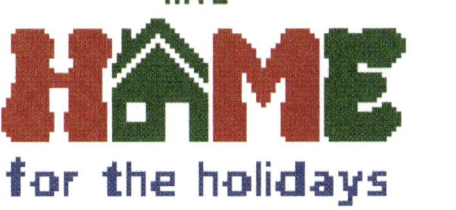

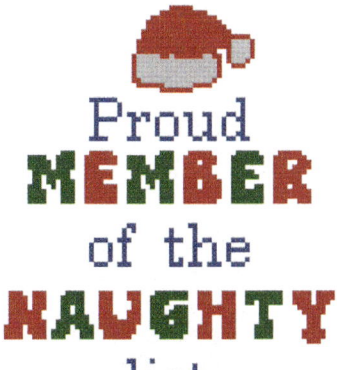

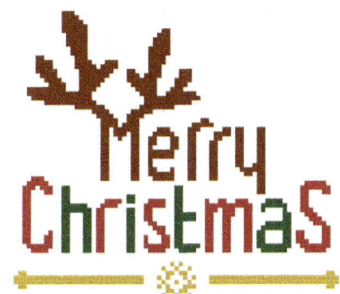

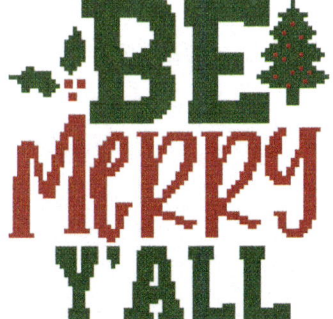

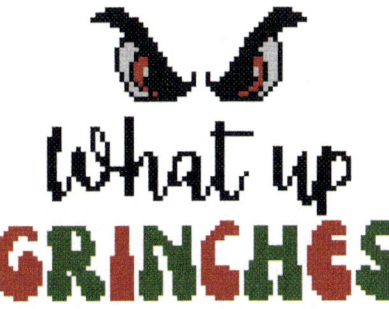

Cross-Stitch Basics

Cross-stitch is a timeless and relaxing embroidery technique that involves stitching small X-shaped stitches onto fabric to create beautiful patterns. If you're new to cross-stitch, this guide will walk you through the essential materials, techniques, and tips to help you get started.

Choosing the Right Fabric

The most common fabric for cross-stitch is Aida cloth, which is woven with evenly spaced holes, making it perfect for beginners. Here are some common fabric options:

- Aida Fabric: Available in different counts (e.g., 14-count, 16-count, 18-count), where the count refers to the number of squares per inch. A lower count (e.g., 14) means larger holes and easier stitching.

- Evenweave Fabric: A smoother fabric with a more delicate appearance, often used for detailed projects. It requires stitching over two threads instead of one.

- Linen Fabric: A high-quality, natural fiber fabric that provides a sophisticated look but requires careful stitching over two threads.

Understanding Aida Fabric

The patterns in this book are designed for 14-count Aida fabric, which means there are 14 stitches per inch. This fabric count is widely used because it offers a good balance between stitch detail and ease of use.

When working with Aida 14, it is recommended to use two strands of embroidery floss for cross-stitches. This provides good coverage without making the stitches too thick. If you prefer a more delicate look, you can experiment with using just one strand.

Aida fabric is available in many colors. If you're a beginner, a light-colored fabric (such as white or cream) is usually easier to work with because the holes are more visible, and the stitches stand out better.

How Fabric Count Affects Design Size

Since these patterns are created for 14-count Aida, using a different fabric count will change the final size of the design.
For example:

- If you use 18-count Aida, the design will be smaller because there are more stitches per inch (18 stitches instead of 14).
- If you use 11-count Aida, the design will be larger because there are fewer stitches per inch.

To calculate the new size of a design on a different fabric count, use this formula:
New width = (Original width in stitches) ÷ (New fabric count) = Size in inches
New height = (Original height in stitches) ÷ (New fabric count) = Size in inches

For example, if a design measures 140 stitches wide by 140 stitches high on 14-count Aida:
On 18-count Aida, it would be 140 ÷ 18 ≈ 7.8 inches wide.
On 11-count Aida, it would be 140 ÷ 11 ≈ 12.7 inches wide.

Choosing a higher-count fabric will make your design more compact and detailed, while a lower-count fabric will make it larger and more spaced out.

How to Cross-Stitch

Follow these simple steps to start your first cross-stitch project:

Prepare the Fabric

- Cut the fabric, leaving extra space around the design to allow for framing.
- Find the center of the fabric by folding it in half twice.
- Mark the center lightly with a pencil or place a small stitch.

Thread the Needle

- Cut a piece of embroidery floss about 18 inches (45 cm) long.
- Separate the strands (most patterns use 2 or 3 strands).
- Thread the needle and either knot the end or use the loop method for a neater start.

Making a Cross-Stitch

- Bring the needle up from the back of the fabric at the starting point.
- Move diagonally to create the first half of the X.
- Bring the needle back up and cross over to complete the stitch.
- Each cross-stitch consists of two diagonal stitches forming an "X." Always keep your top stitches slanting in the same direction for a neat and uniform look.

Following the Pattern

- Read the chart carefully, matching the symbols to the floss colors.
- Start from the center of the pattern and work outward.
- Use even tension to keep stitches uniform.

Secure Your Thread Without Knots

Instead of tying knots, weave the thread under a few completed stitches at the back of your work. Knots can create bumps and make framing difficult.

Useful Stitching Techniques

- Loop Start Method (for 2 strands): If you're using an even number of strands (like 2 strands on 14-count Aida), fold a single strand in half and thread both ends through the needle. Bring the needle up from the back, leaving a small loop. When you make your first stitch, pass the needle through the loop to secure it.

- Backstitching: Some patterns use backstitching for outlines or fine details. This is done with a simple running stitch, usually using one strand of floss.

Essential Tools for a Better Stitching Experience

To make your stitching more enjoyable, consider using these tools:

- Embroidery Hoop or Frame – Keeps the fabric taut and makes stitching easier.
- Sharp Embroidery Scissors – Helps cut threads cleanly.
- Thread Organizer – Keeps your embroidery floss neat and tangle-free.
- Good Lighting and Magnifier – Reduces eye strain, especially for detailed work.

Now that you know the basics, you're ready to start stitching! Enjoy the process, and most importantly—**have fun!**

Contents

12	Ho Ho Ho Pour the Merlot
13	Dear Santa, I can explain
14	Dear Santa, I really tried
15	Dear Santa, it's a long story
16	Christmas baking crew
17	Sweet but twisted
18	I just want to watch Christmas movies
19	Have yourself a merry little Christmas
20	Dear Santa #no regrets
21	Dear Santa, it was my sister
22	I sleigh
23	Holiday baking team
24	May joy fill your home and peace find it's way to you this season
25	Christmas calories don't count
26	Believe in Santa
27	Santa stop here
28	Rudolph is my bestie
29	Christmas loading
30	What the elf?
31	Santa's favorite
32	Milk and cookies for Santa
33	Let it snow somewhere else
34	Full of holiday spirit aka rum
35	Full of holiday spirit aka wine
36	Full of holiday spirit aka vodka
37	Dear Santa, it was just a phase
38	I am freaking jolly
39	Cookie baking crew
40	Don't get your tinsel in a tangle
41	Chilling with my snowmies
42	Dear Santa, it was the dog

43 Dear Santa, it was the cat
44 Santa's little sweetie
45 But first let me take an elfie
46 Official North Pole elf team
47 Merry and bright
48 Christmas chaos coordinator
49 Christmas vibes
50 Merry merry merry Christmas
51 We wish you a merry Christmas
52 There is no place like home for the holidays
53 What up grinches?
54 Joy to the world
55 Dear Santa, I've been good
56 Dabbing through the snow
57 Believe in the magic of Christmas
58 Dear Santa, it was framed
59 Will trade brother for presents
60 Dear Santa, will trade sister for presents
61 Nice with a hint of naughty
62 It's Christmas time
63 Merry Christmas
64 Be merry y'all
65 Sleigh girl sleigh
66 Proud member of the naughty list
67 Christmas crew
68 Bottoms up
69 Merry Christmas
70 Santa's sidekick
71 Dear Santa, the wine made me do it
72 Merry Christmas
73 Be jolly
74 With love from Santa
75 Merry Christmas
76 Ho Ho Ho

Legend:

◆ DMC 817 coral red - vy dk

♣ DMC 319 pistachio green - vy dk

Legend:

◇ DMC 817 coral red - vy dk   ♣ DMC 319 pistachio green - vy dk

13

Legend:

◆ DMC 817 coral red - vy dk   ♣ DMC 319 pistachio green - vy dk

Legend:

◇ DMC 817 coral red - vy dk   ♣ DMC 319 pistachio green - vy dk

Legend:

◆ DMC 817 coral red - vy dk

♣ DMC 319 pistachio green - vy dk

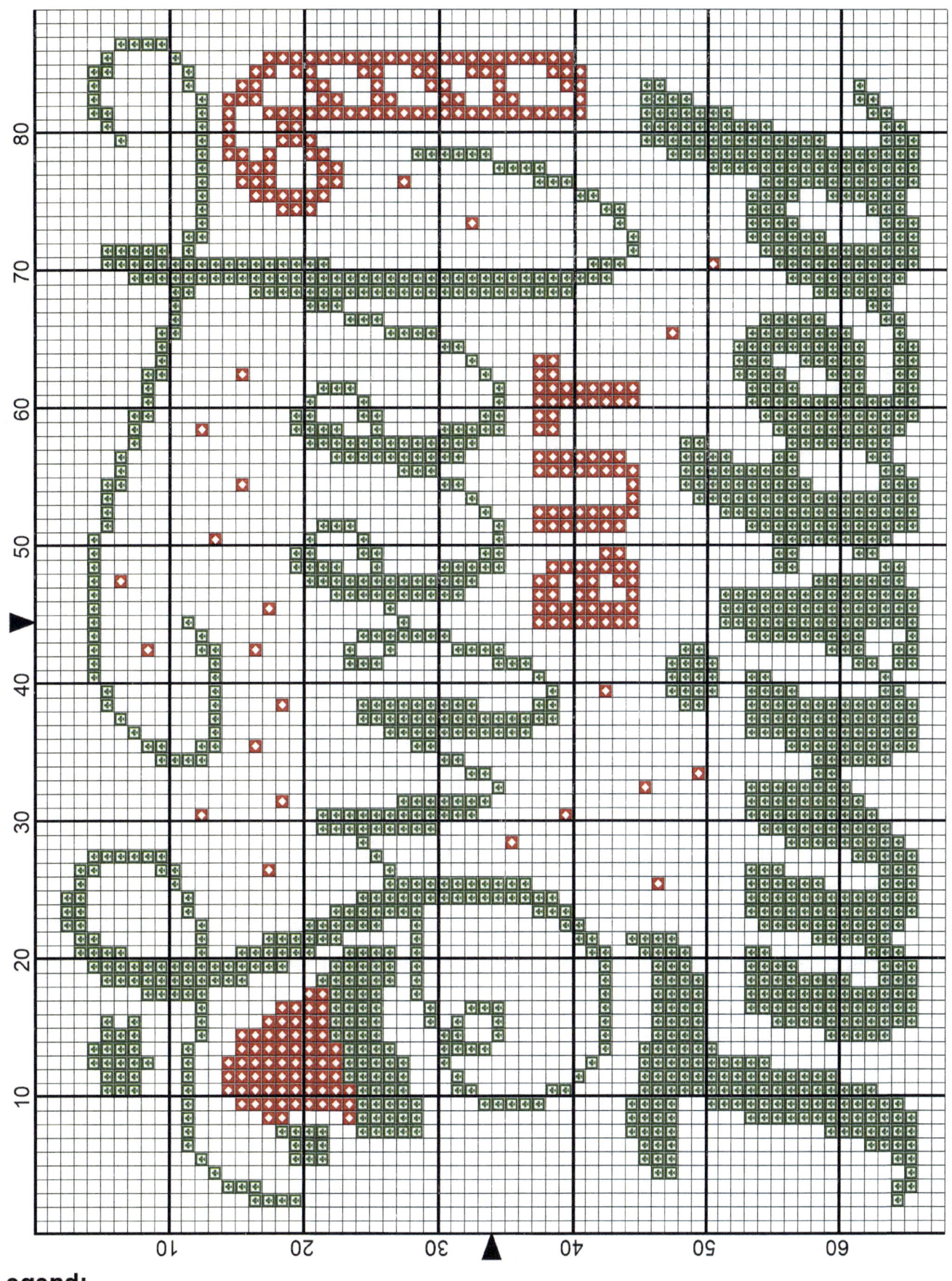

Legend:

◆ DMC 817 coral red - vy dk   ♣ DMC 319 pistachio green - vy dk

17

Legend:

◇ DMC 817 coral red - vy dk
♣ DMC 319 pistachio green - vy dk

Legend:

◆ DMC   817   coral red - vy dk   ♣ DMC   319   pistachio green - vy dk

Legend:

◆ DMC   817   coral red - vy dk   ♣ DMC   319   pistachio green - vy dk

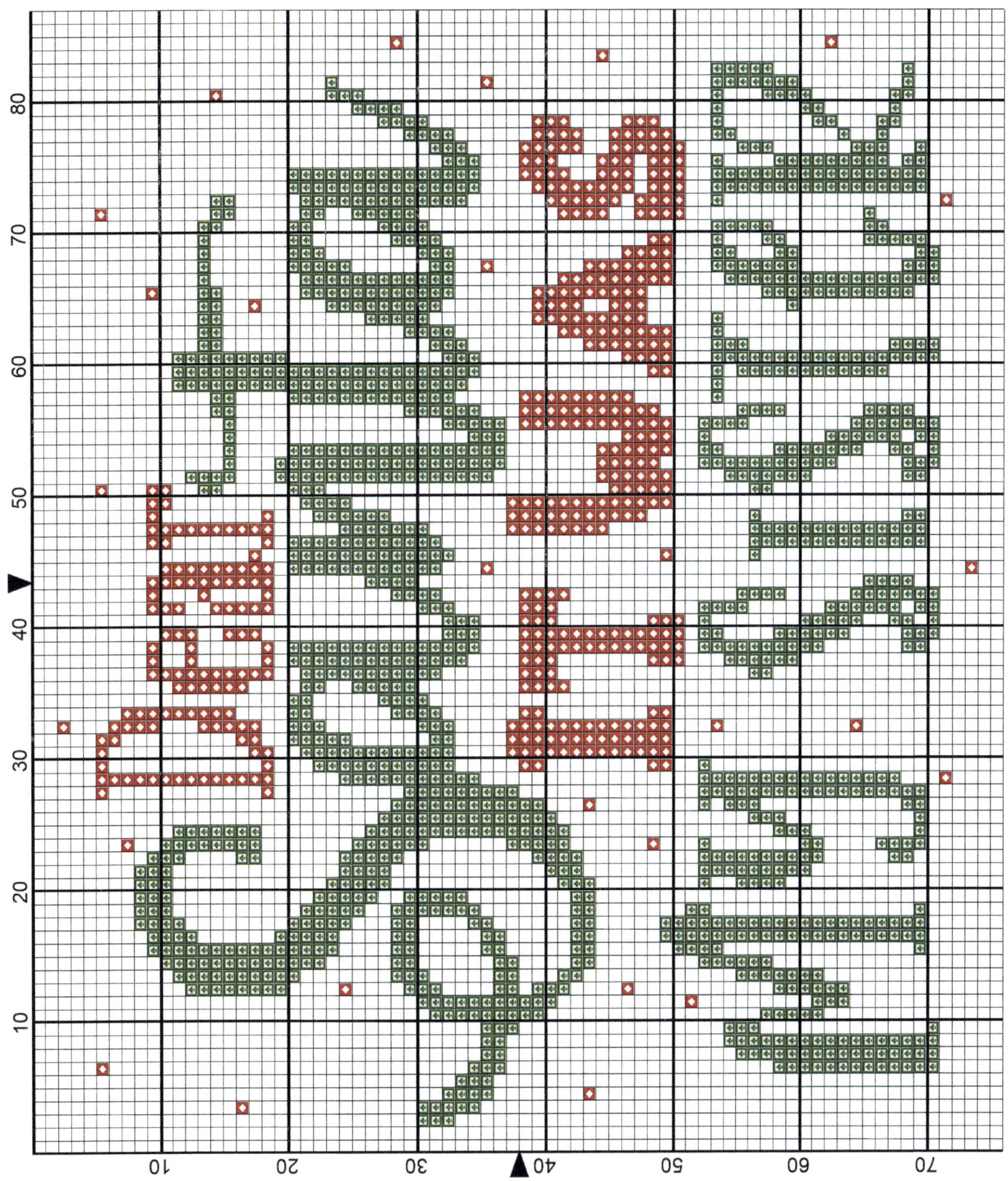

Legend:

◆ DMC 817 coral red - vy dk ♣ DMC 319 pistachio green - vy dk

21

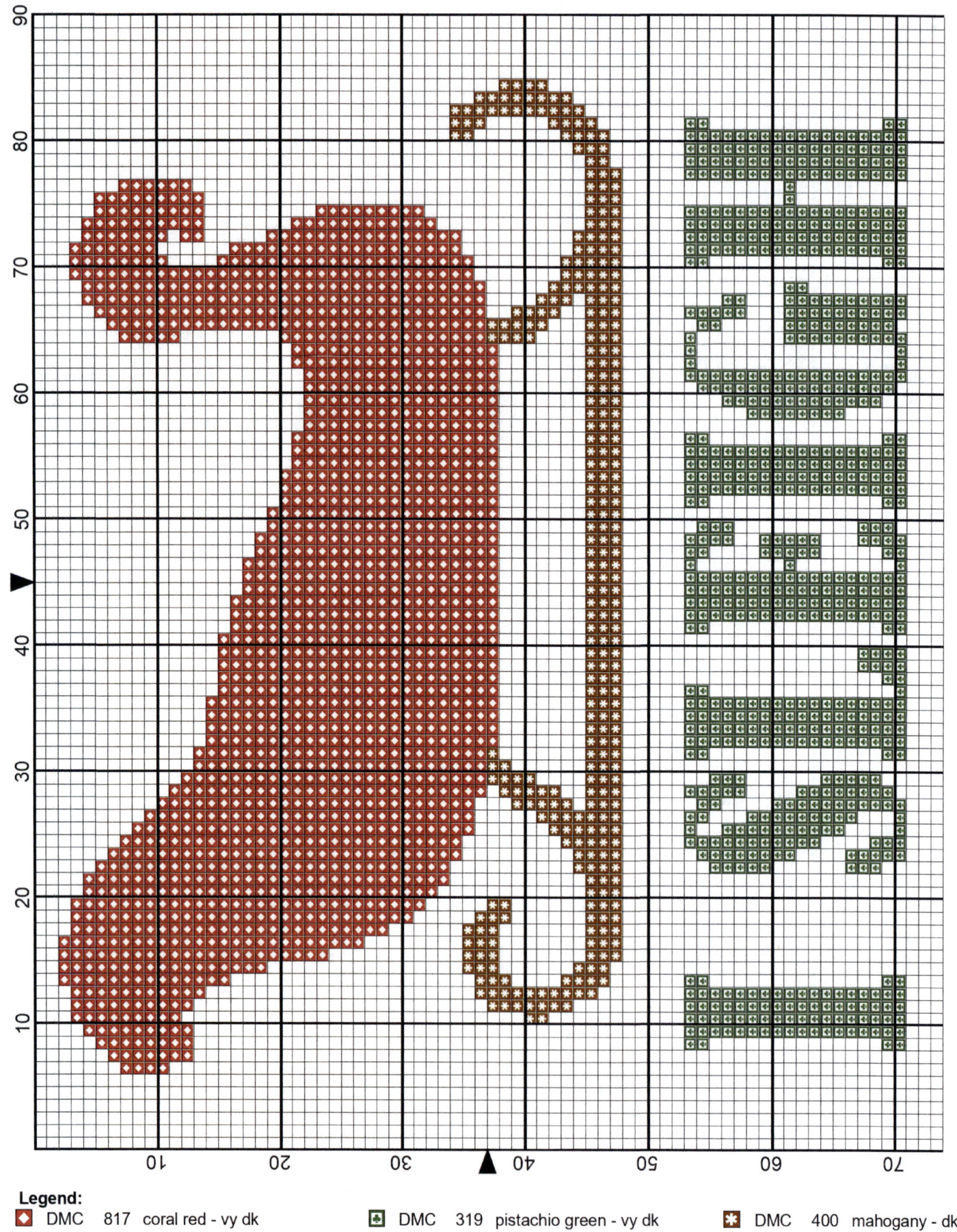

Legend:
- DMC 817 coral red - vy dk
- DMC 319 pistachio green - vy dk
- DMC 400 mahogany - dk

22

Legend:

	DMC	817	coral red - vy dk		DMC	437	tan - lt
	DMC	319	pistachio green - vy dk		DMC	Ecru	ecru

Legend:

◆ DMC 817 coral red - vy dk   ♣ DMC 319 pistachio green - vy dk

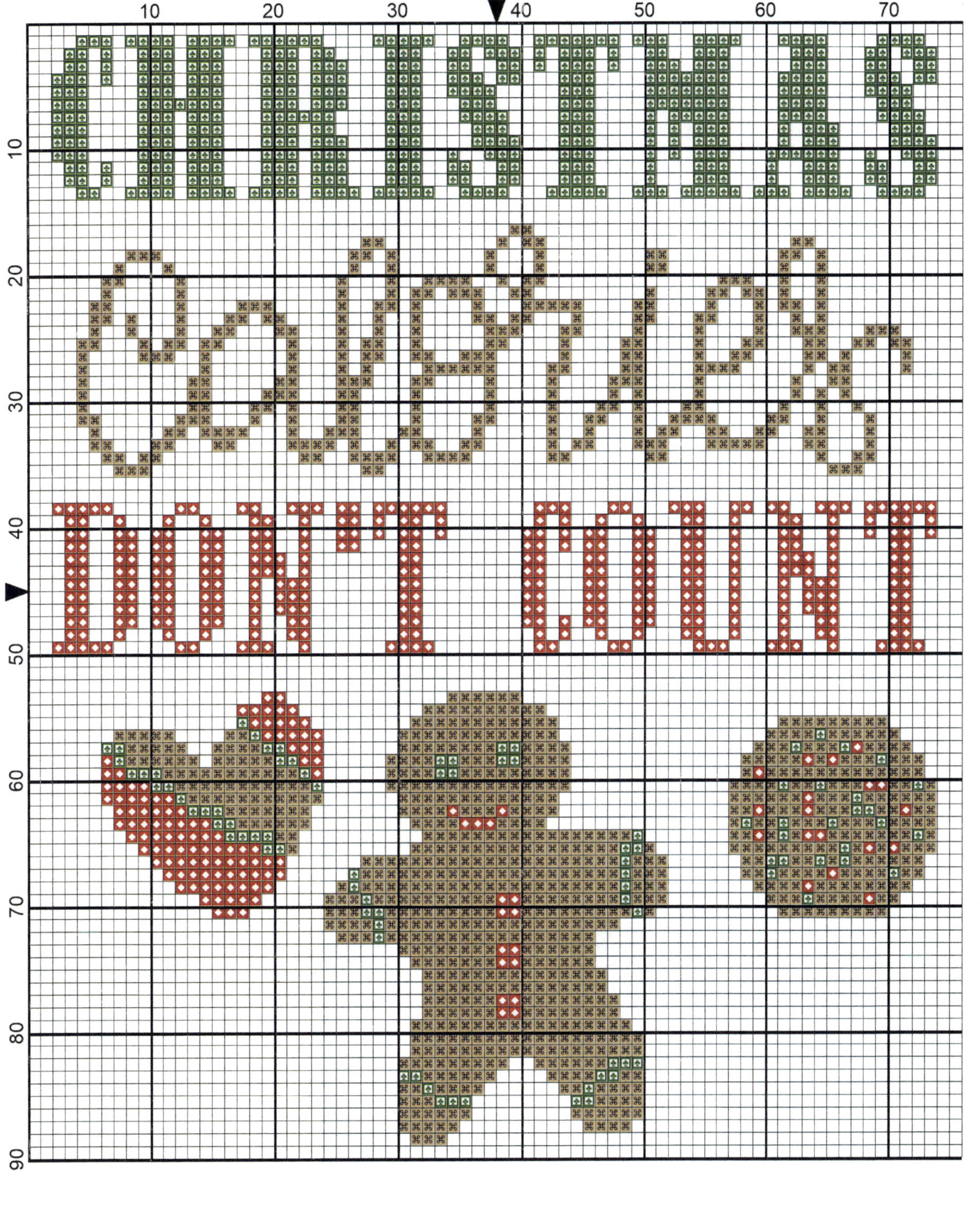

25

Legend:

	DMC	817	coral red - vy dk
	DMC	798	delft blue - dk
	DMC	319	pistachio green - vy dk
	DMC	Ecru	ecru

Legend:

 DMC 817 coral red - vy dk ☐ DMC 310 black

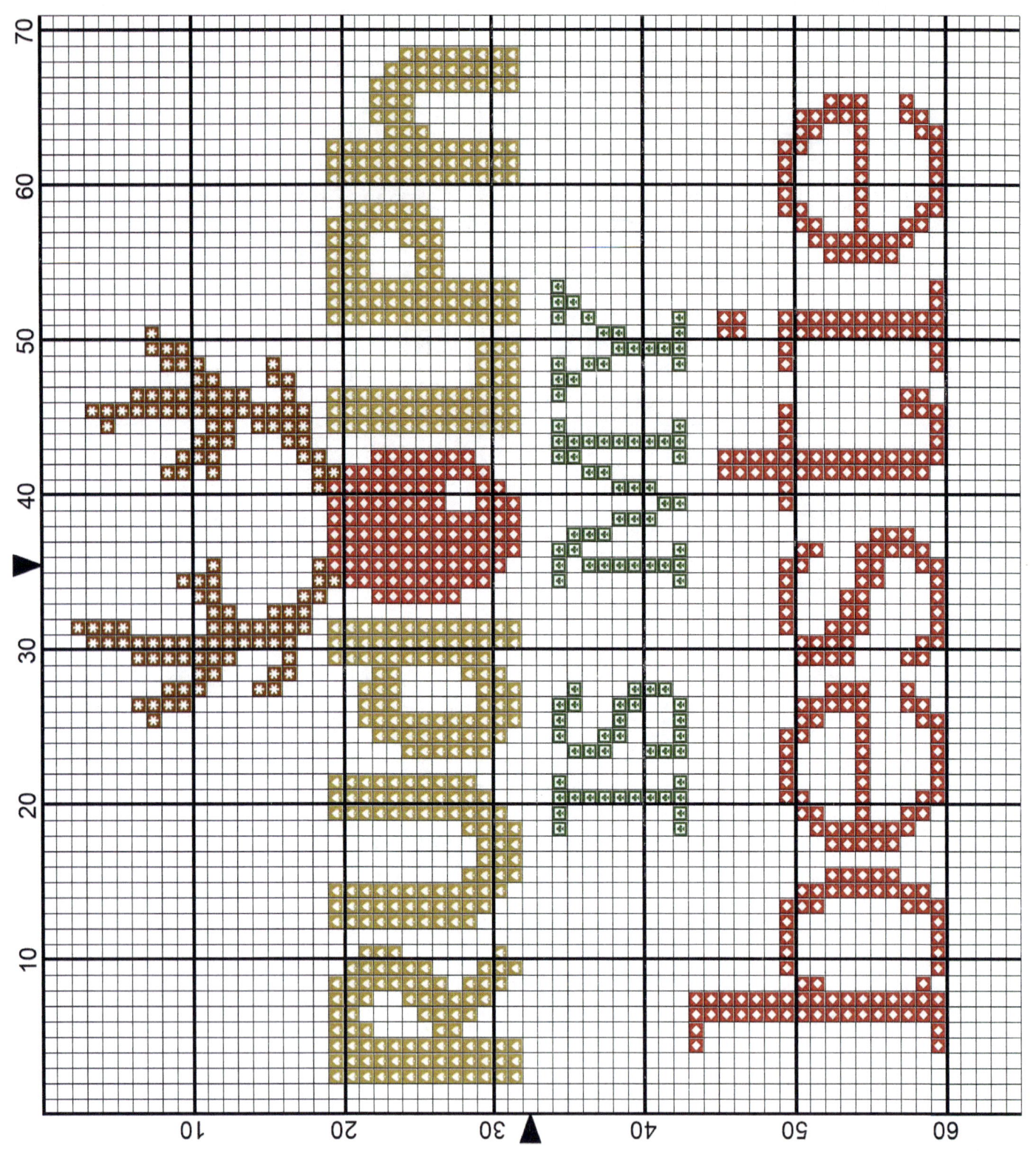

Legend:

	DMC	817	coral red - vy dk		DMC	3828	hazel nut brown
	DMC	319	pistachio green - vy dk		DMC	400	mahogany - dk

Legend:
- DMC 817 coral red - vy dk
- DMC 798 delft blue - dk
- DMC 319 pistachio green - vy dk
- DMC 728 golden yellow
- DMC 310 black

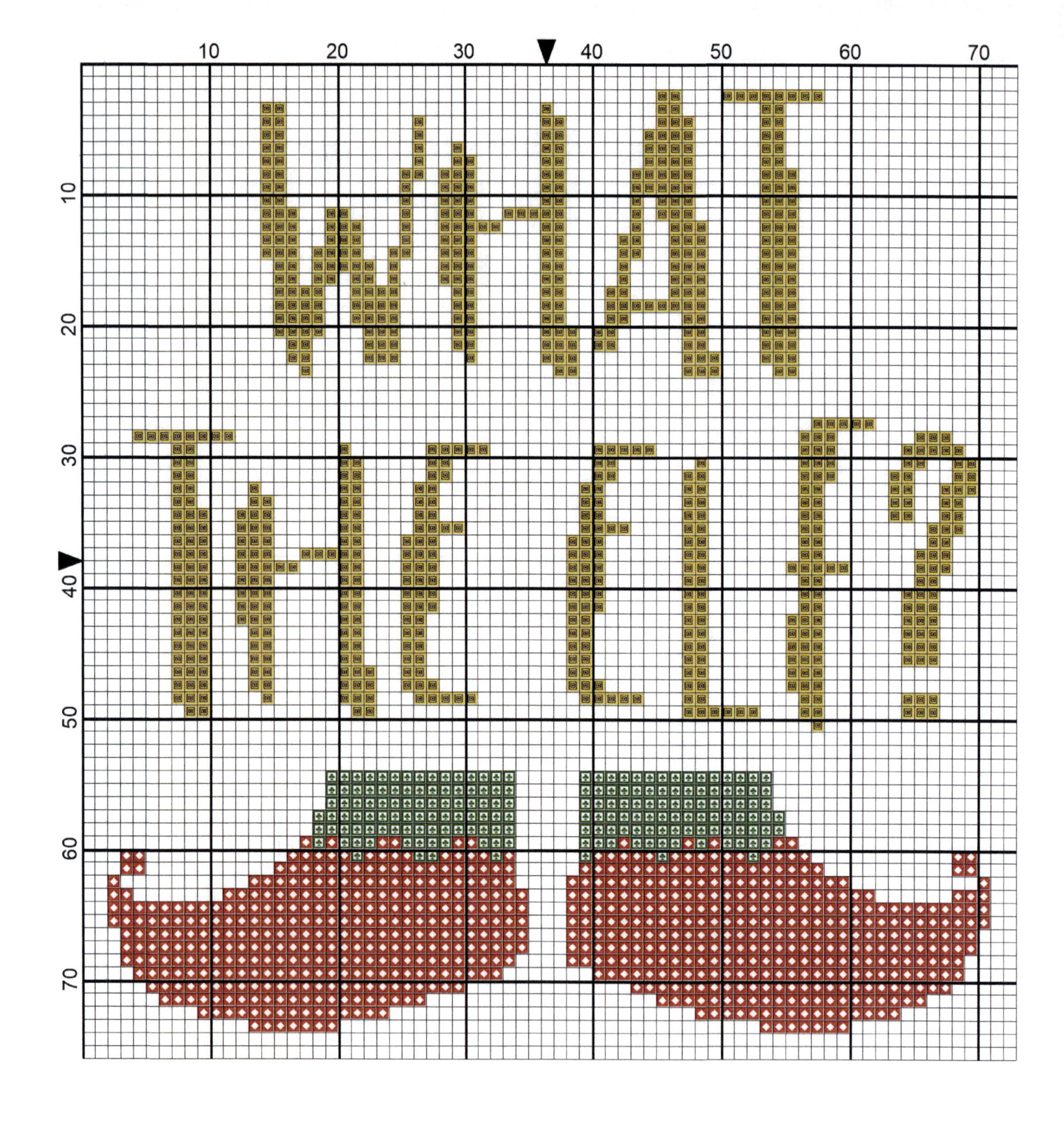

Legend:
- ◆ DMC 817 coral red - vy dk
- ♣ DMC 319 pistachio green - vy dk
- ▣ DMC 728 golden yellow

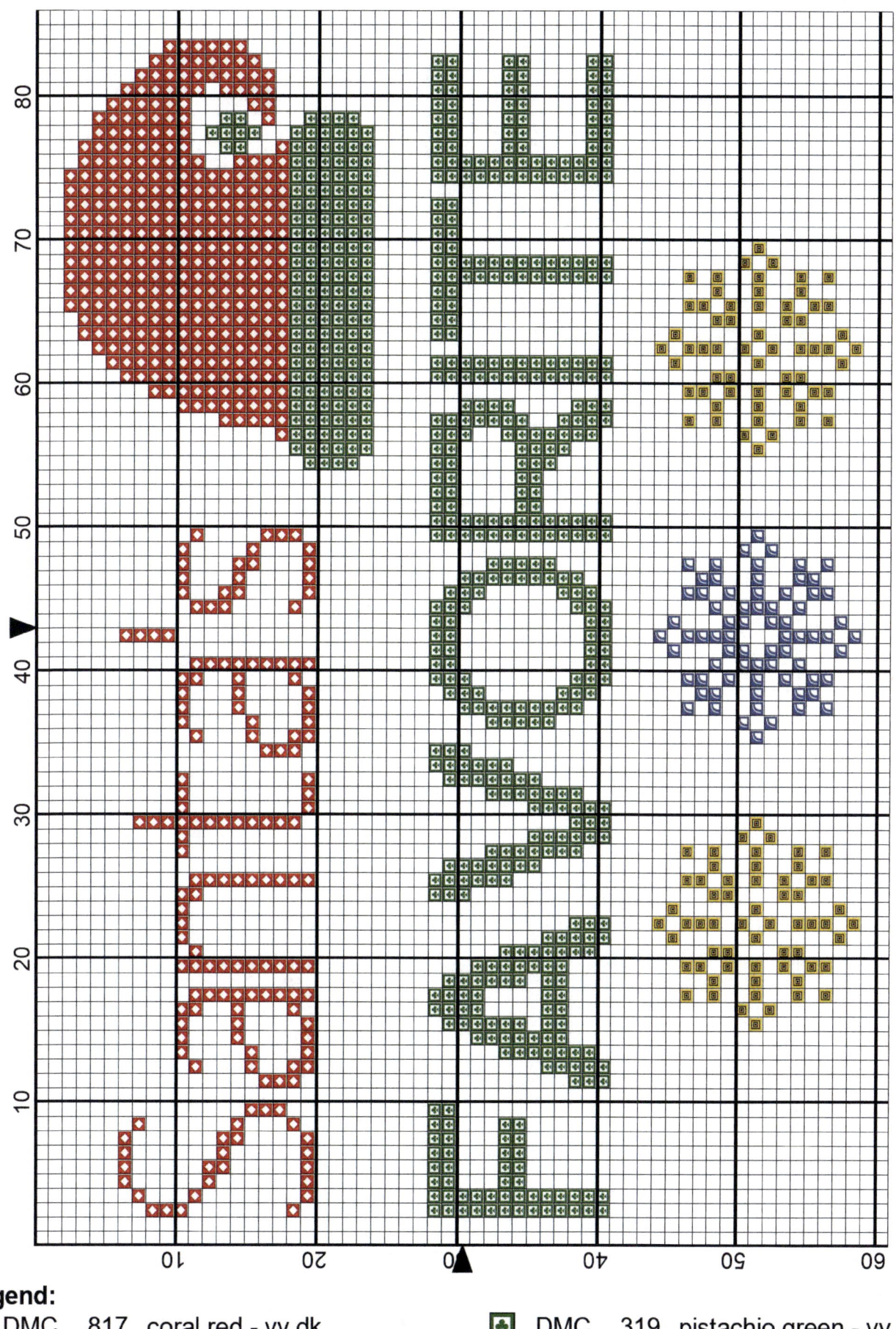

Legend:

	DMC	817	coral red - vy dk
	DMC	798	delft blue - dk
	DMC	319	pistachio green - vy dk
	DMC	728	golden yellow

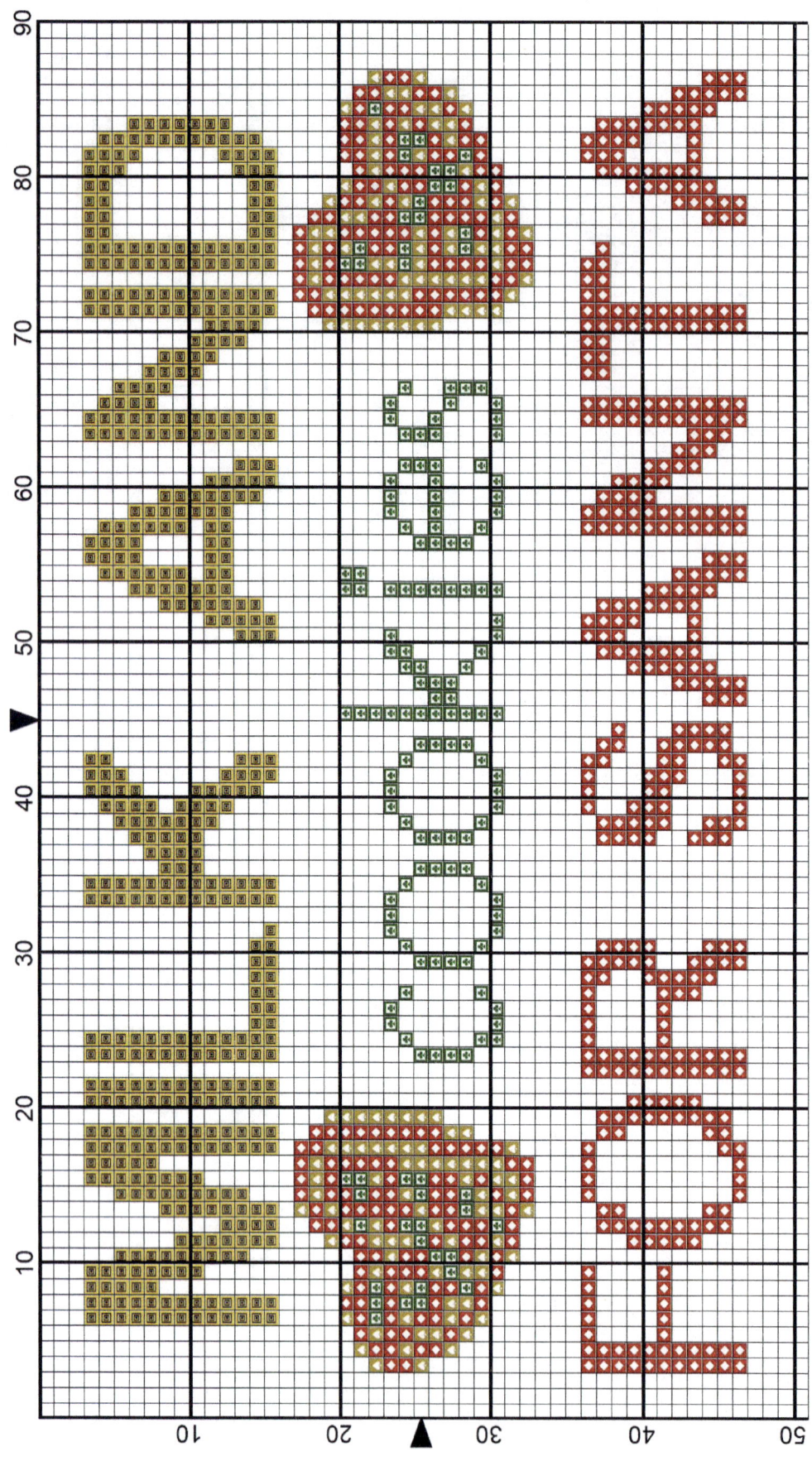

Legend:

	DMC	817	coral red - vy dk		DMC	3828	hazel nut brown
	DMC	319	pistachio green - vy dk		DMC	728	golden yellow

Legend:

◇ DMC 817 coral red - vy dk ♣ DMC 319 pistachio green - vy dk

Legend:

◆ DMC   817   coral red - vy dk   ♣ DMC   319   pistachio green - vy dk

Legend:

◇ DMC 817 coral red - vy dk 🍀 DMC 319 pistachio green - vy dk

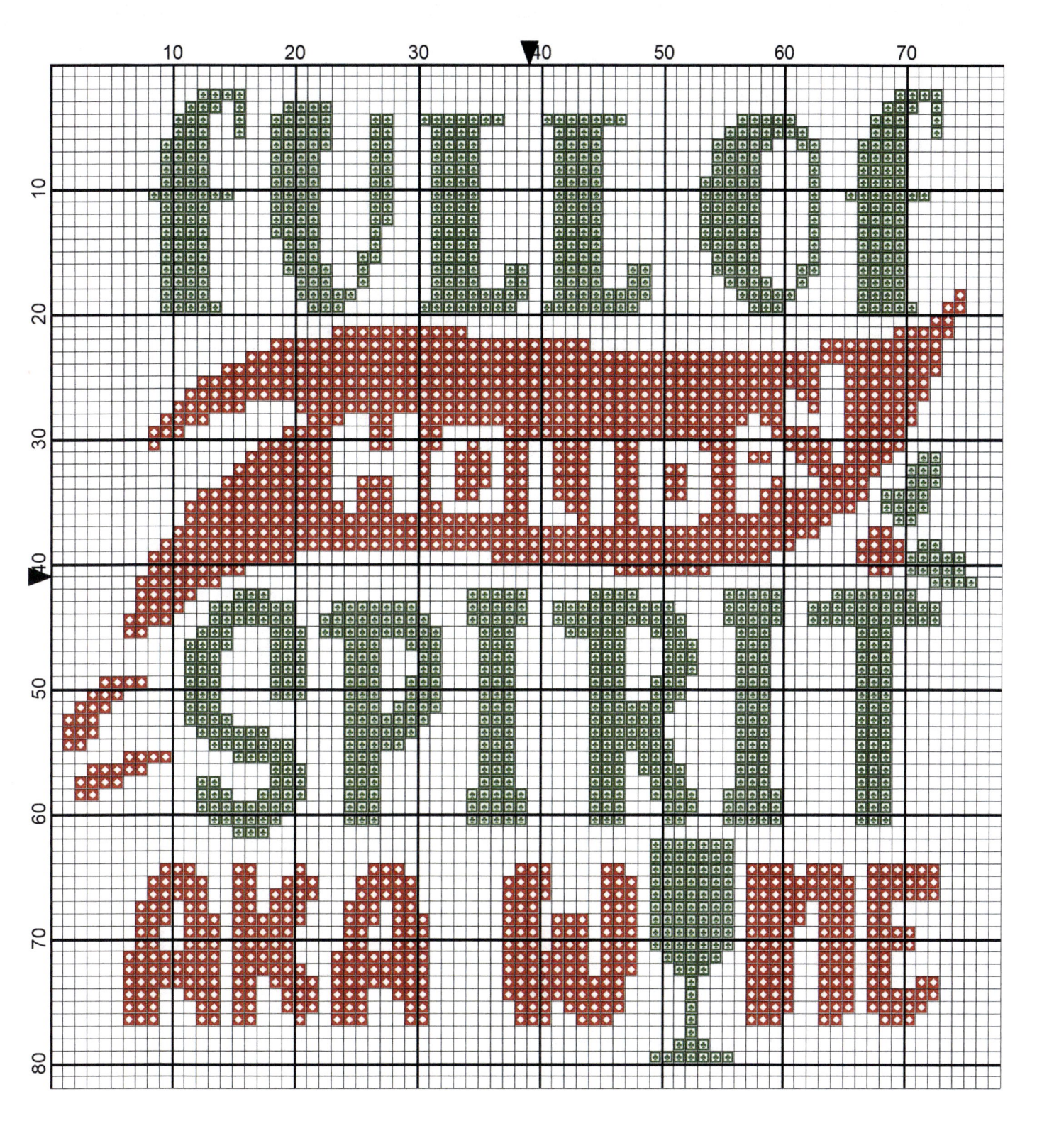

Legend:

◆ DMC 817 coral red - vy dk   ♣ DMC 319 pistachio green - vy dk

Legend:

◆ DMC 817 coral red - vy dk   ♣ DMC 319 pistachio green - vy dk

Legend:

◇ DMC 817 coral red - vy dk   ♣ DMC 319 pistachio green - vy dk

Legend:

◆ DMC 817 coral red - vy dk

♣ DMC 319 pistachio green - vy dk

Legend:

◆ DMC 817 coral red - vy dk ♣ DMC 319 pistachio green - vy dk

40

Legend:

◆ DMC 817 coral red - vy dk   ♣ DMC 319 pistachio green - vy dk

41

Legend:

◆ DMC 817 coral red - vy dk　　　♣ DMC 319 pistachio green - vy dk

Legend:

◆ DMC 817 coral red - vy dk

♣ DMC 319 pistachio green - vy dk

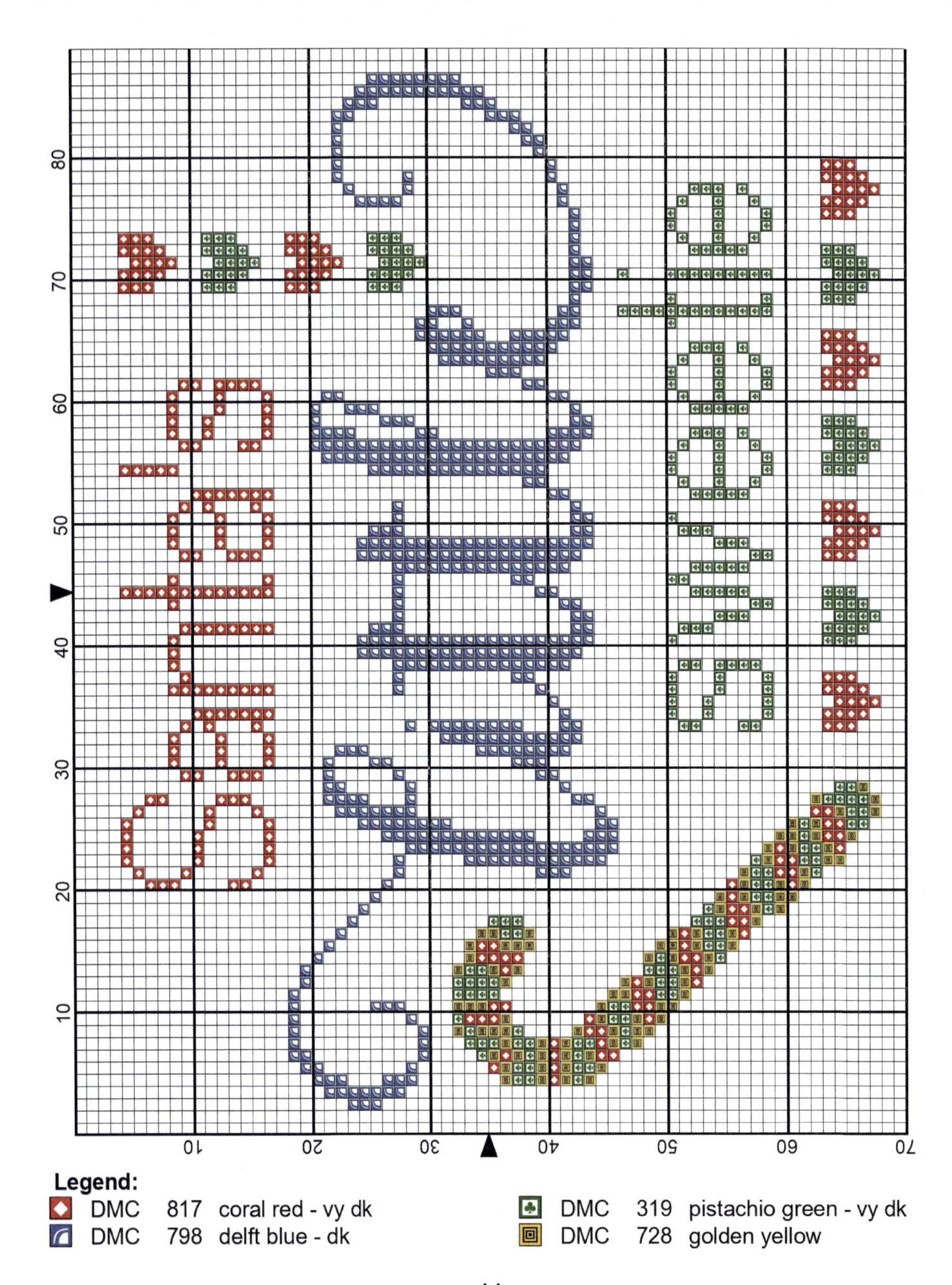

Legend:

- ◆ DMC 817 coral red - vy dk
- ◪ DMC 798 delft blue - dk
- ♣ DMC 319 pistachio green - vy dk
- ▣ DMC 728 golden yellow

44

Legend:

- ◆ DMC 817 coral red - vy dk
- ◖ DMC 798 delft blue - dk
- ♣ DMC 319 pistachio green - vy dk
- ▣ DMC 728 golden yellow

45

Legend:
- DMC 817 coral red - vy dk
- DMC 798 delft blue - dk
- DMC 319 pistachio green - vy dk

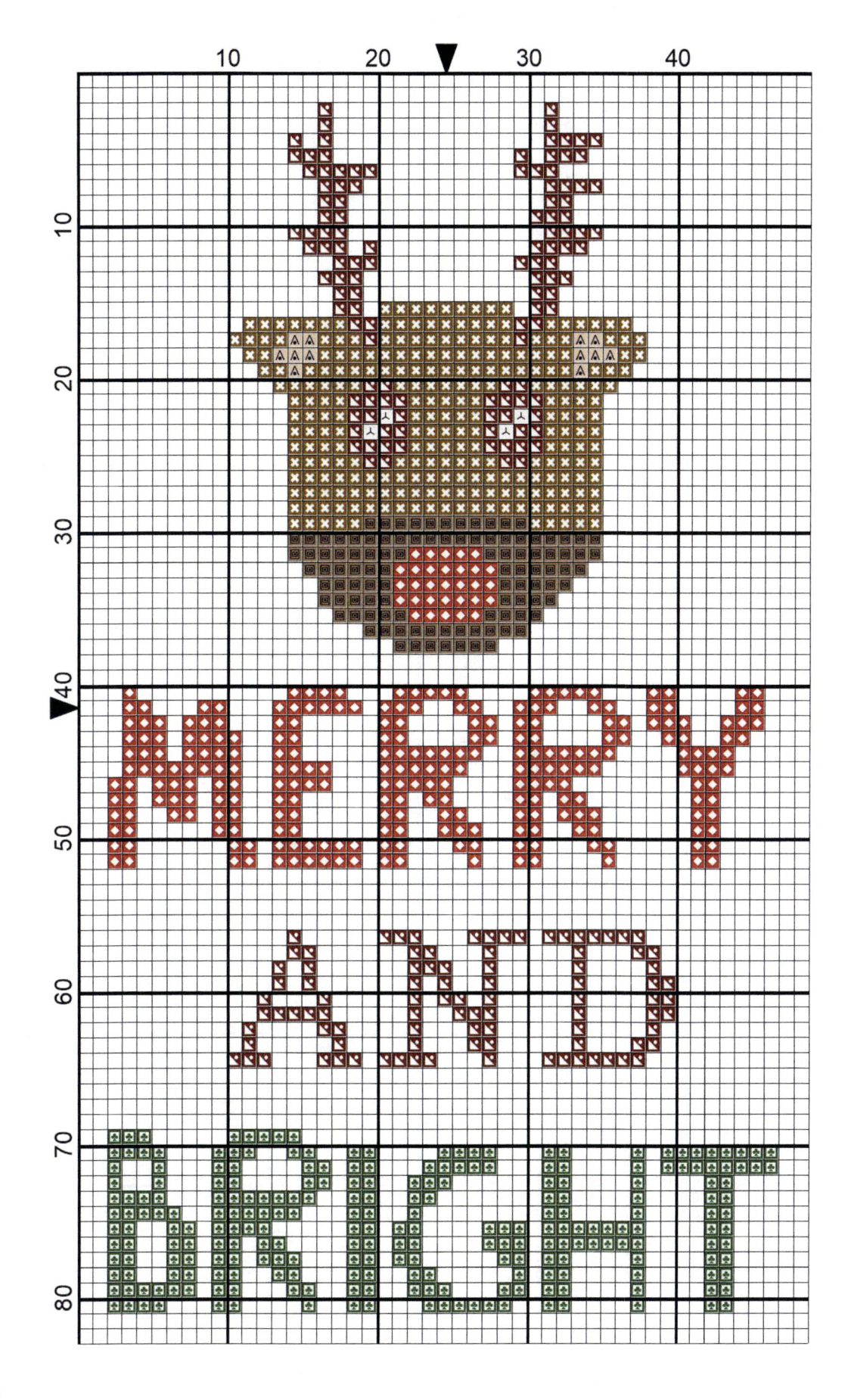

Legend:

	DMC	817	coral red - vy dk
	DMC	319	pistachio green - vy dk
	DMC	3857	rosewood - dk

	DMC	950	desert sand - lt
	DMC	3772	desert sand - vy dk
	DMC	434	brown - lt

	DMC	Ecru	ecru

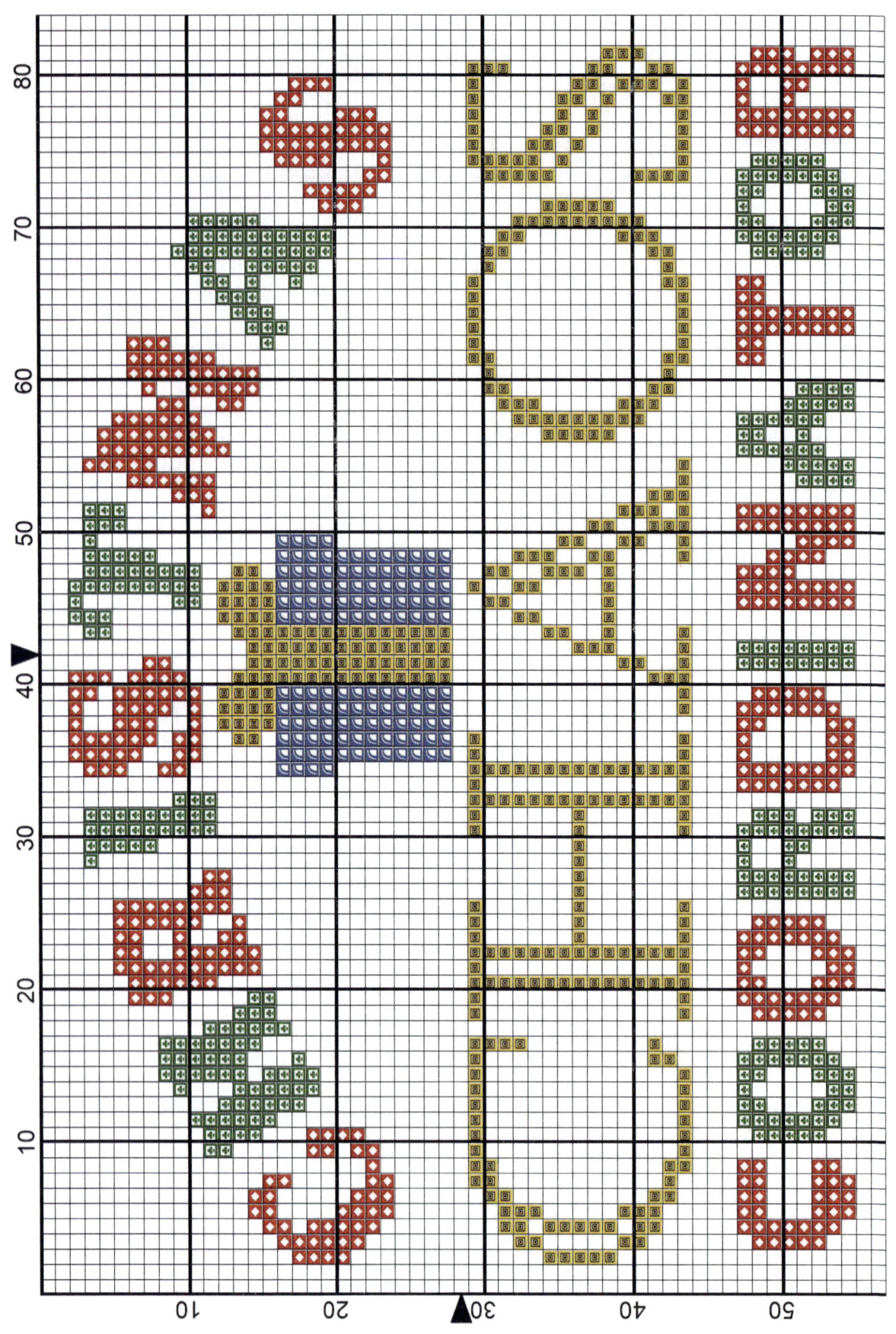

Legend:

	DMC	817	coral red - vy dk		DMC	319	pistachio green - vy dk
	DMC	798	delft blue - dk		DMC	728	golden yellow

Legend:

	DMC	817	coral red - vy dk		DMC	319	pistachio green - vy dk		DMC	3882	cocoa - md lt
	DMC	798	delft blue - dk		DMC	728	golden yellow				

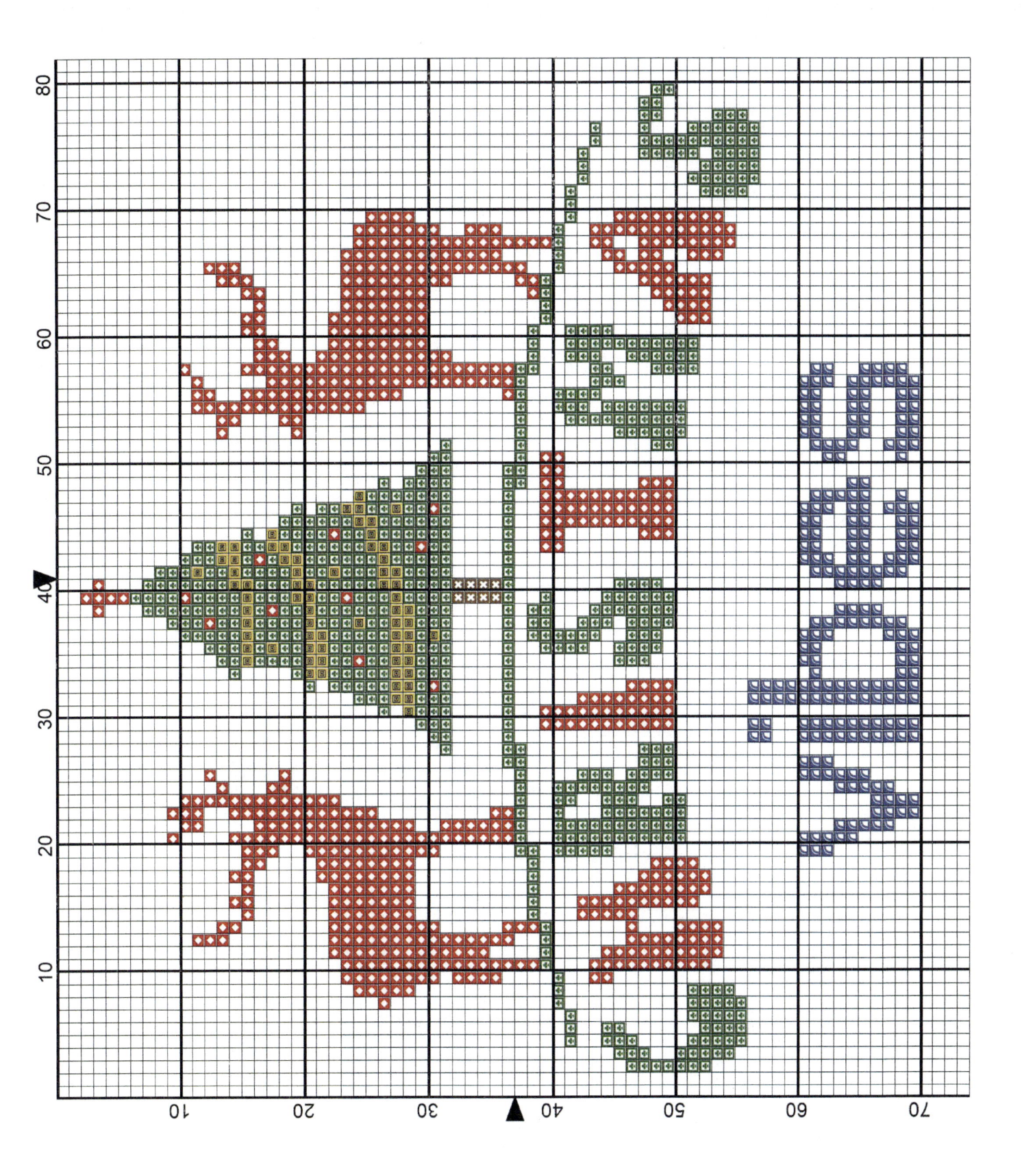

Legend:

	DMC	817	coral red - vy dk
	DMC	798	delft blue - dk
	DMC	319	pistachio green - vy dk
	DMC	728	golden yellow

50

Legend:

DMC 798 delft blue - dk   DMC 728 golden yellow

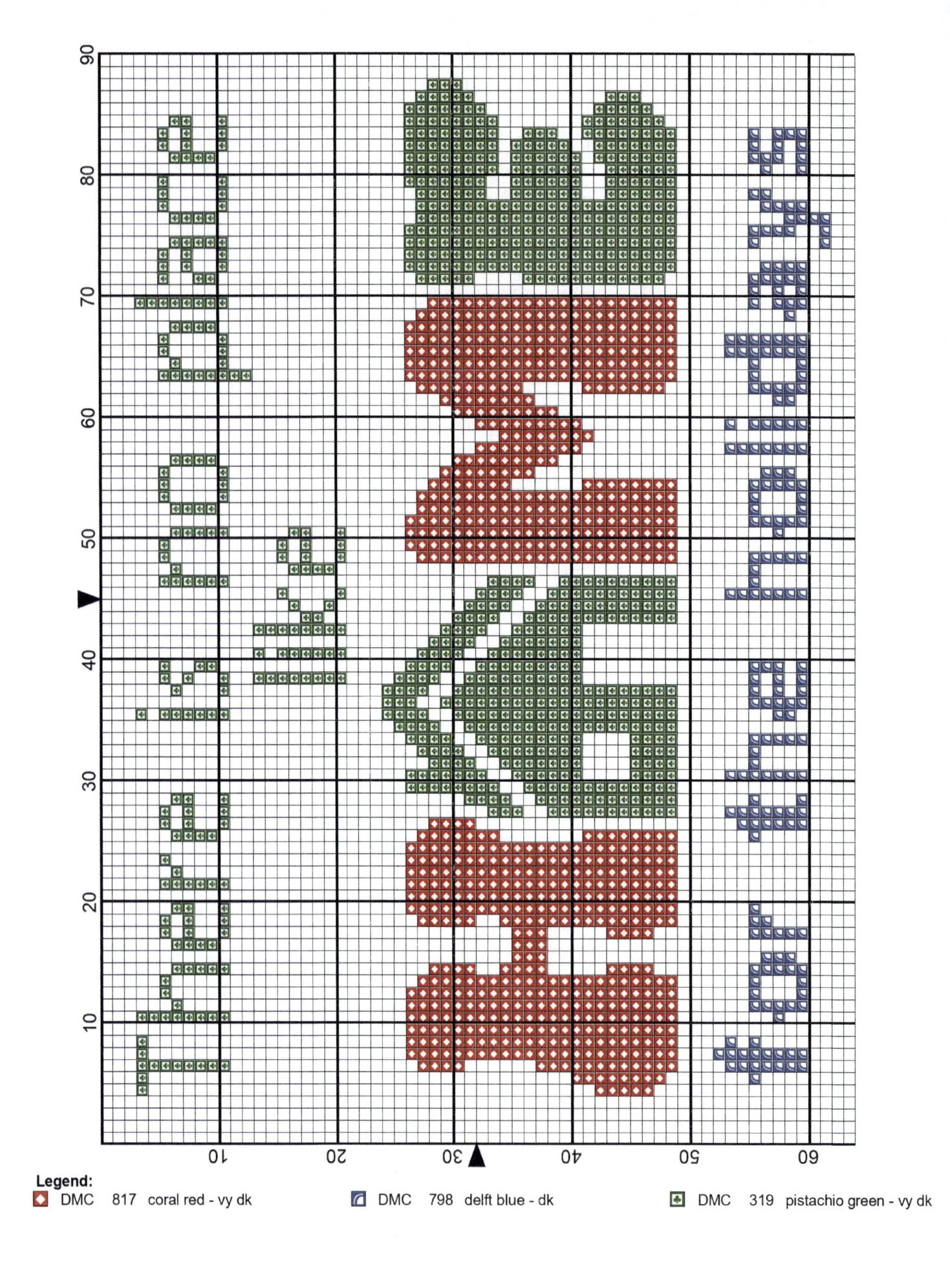

Legend:
- DMC 817 coral red - vy dk
- DMC 798 delft blue - dk
- DMC 319 pistachio green - vy dk

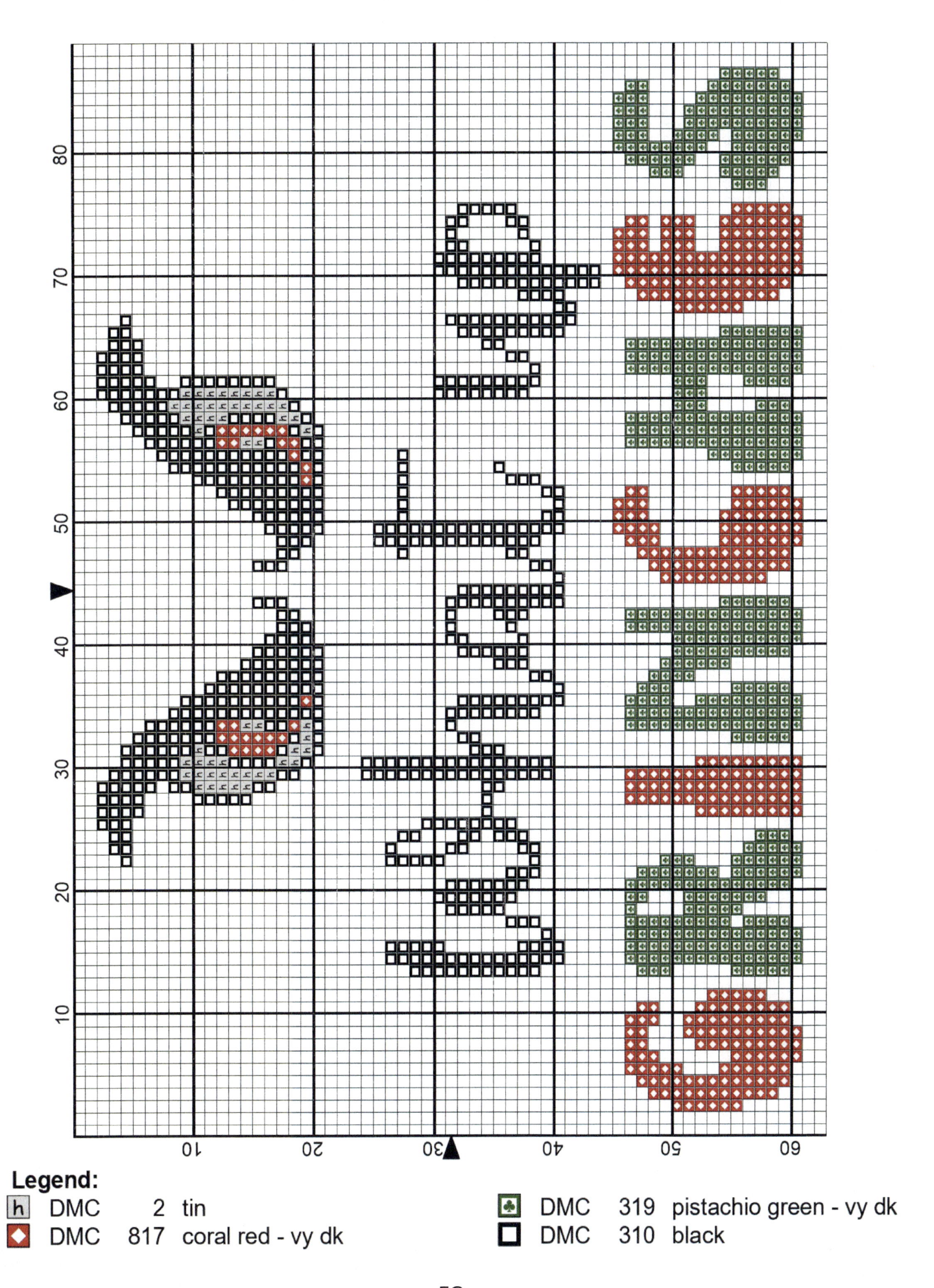

Legend:

	DMC		
h	DMC	2	tin
◆	DMC	817	coral red - vy dk
♣	DMC	319	pistachio green - vy dk
□	DMC	310	black

Legend:

◆ DMC 817 coral red - vy dk   ♣ DMC 319 pistachio green - vy dk

Legend:

◇ DMC 817 coral red - vy dk   ♣ DMC 319 pistachio green - vy dk

Legend:

◆ DMC 817 coral red - vy dk ♣ DMC 319 pistachio green - vy dk

Legend:

◇ DMC 817 coral red - vy dk 　　　♣ DMC 319 pistachio green - vy dk

Legend:

◆ DMC   817   coral red - vy dk   ♣ DMC   319   pistachio green - vy dk

Legend:

◇ DMC 817 coral red - vy dk   ♣ DMC 319 pistachio green - vy dk

Legend:

	DMC	2	tin
	DMC	817	coral red - vy dk
	DMC	798	delft blue - dk
	DMC	319	pistachio green - vy dk
	DMC	728	golden yellow

Legend:

◇ DMC 817 coral red - vy dk   ♣ DMC 319 pistachio green - vy dk

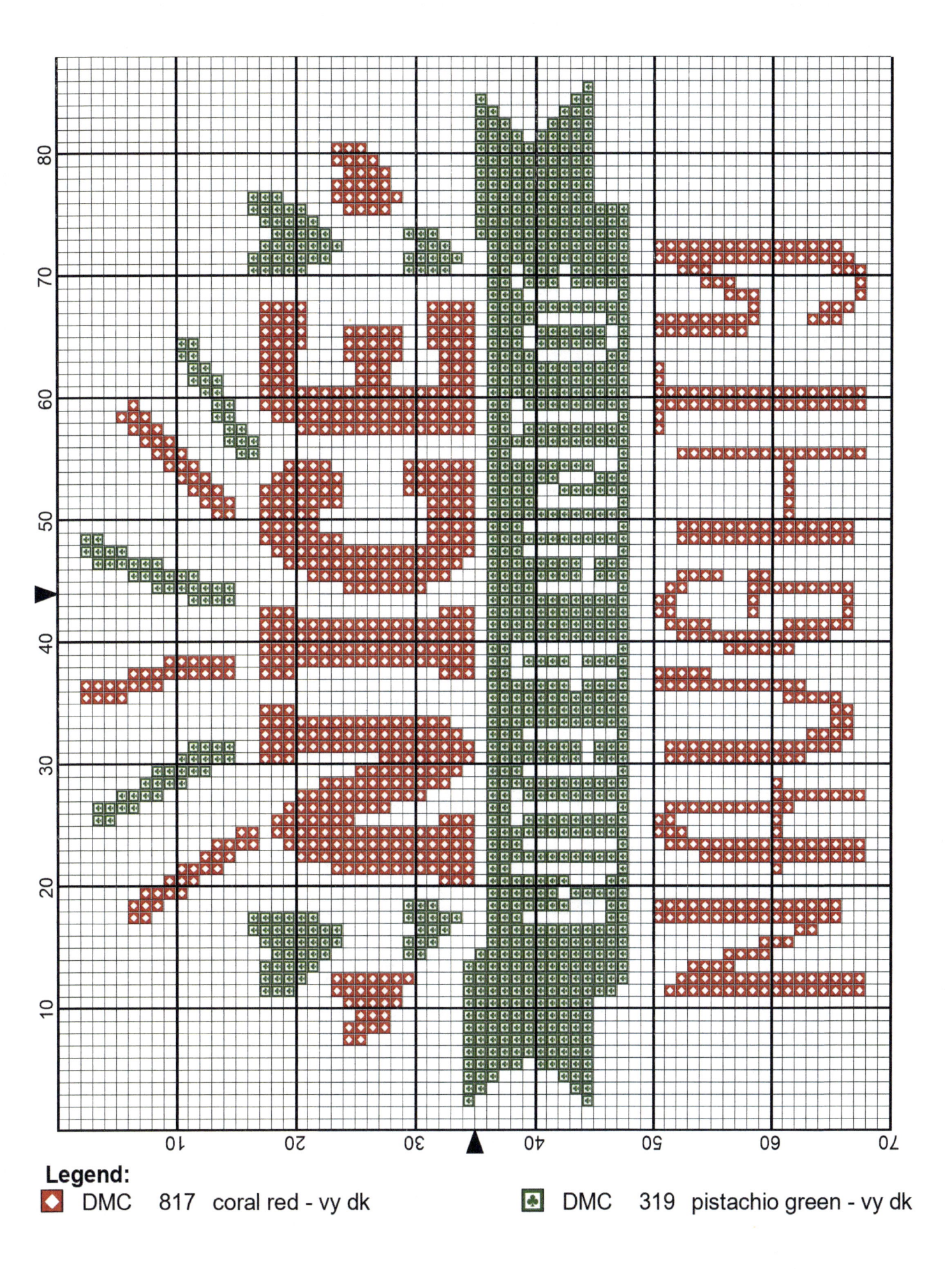

61

Legend:

◆ DMC 817 coral red - vy dk

♣ DMC 319 pistachio green - vy dk

Legend:

	DMC	817	coral red - vy dk		DMC	728	golden yellow
	DMC	319	pistachio green - vy dk		DMC	400	mahogany - dk

Legend:

◇ DMC 817 coral red - vy dk   ♣ DMC 319 pistachio green - vy dk

Legend:

Symbol	DMC	Color
◆	DMC 817	coral red - vy dk
⌒	DMC 798	delft blue - dk
♣	DMC 319	pistachio green - vy dk
▣	DMC 728	golden yellow

Legend:

h	DMC	2	tin
◆	DMC	817	coral red - vy dk
⌐	DMC	798	delft blue - dk
♣	DMC	319	pistachio green - vy dk

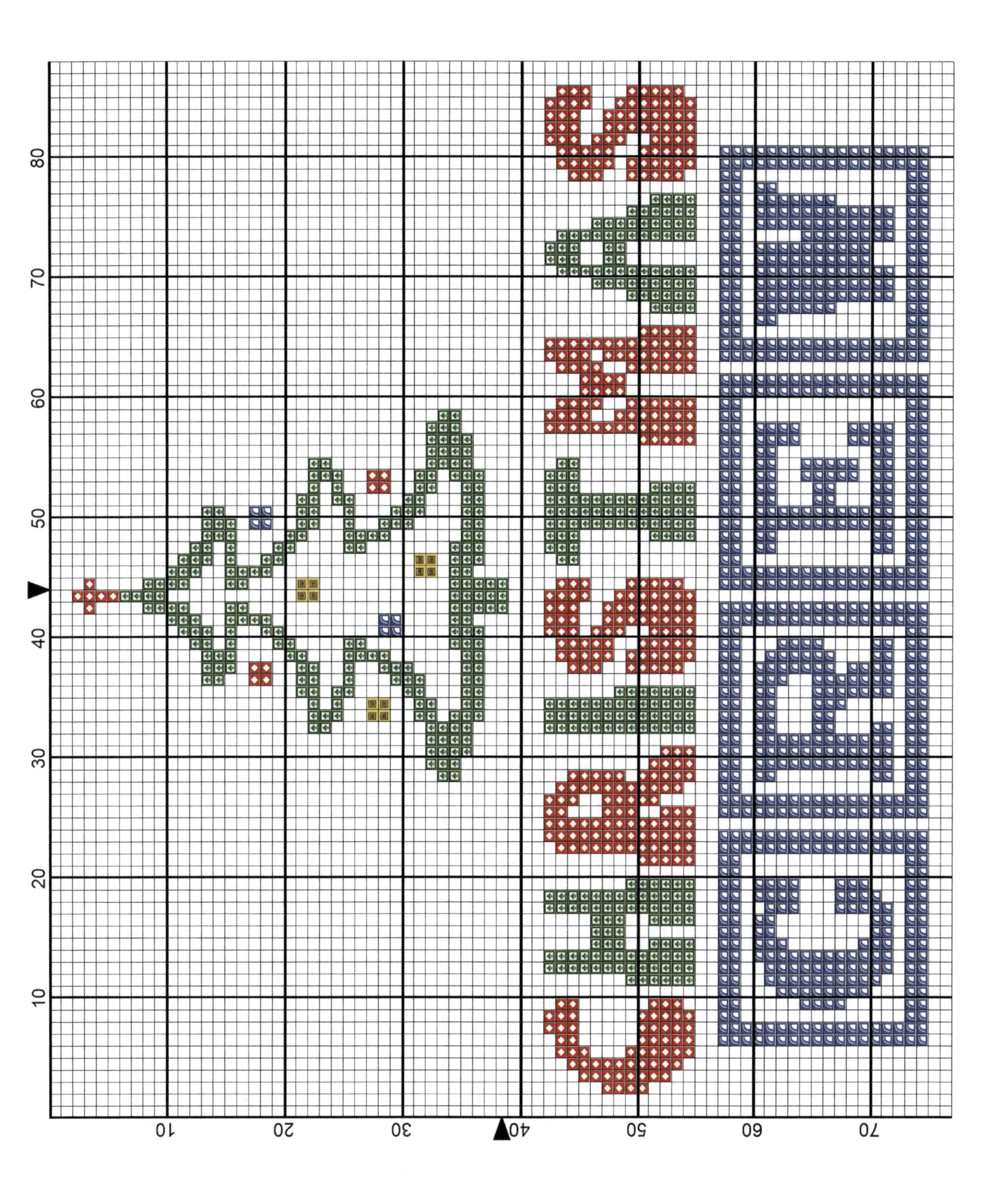

Legend:

	DMC	817	coral red - vy dk		DMC	319	pistachio green - vy dk
	DMC	798	delft blue - dk		DMC	728	golden yellow

Legend:
	DMC	2	tin
	DMC	817	coral red - vy dk
	DMC	798	delft blue - dk
	DMC	319	pistachio green - vy dk
	DMC	728	golden yellow
	DMC	310	black

Legend:
- ◊ DMC 817 coral red - vy dk
- ♣ DMC 319 pistachio green - vy dk
- ✲ DMC 400 mahogany - dk

69

Legend:

Symbol	DMC	Color
◇	DMC 817	coral red - vy dk
♣	DMC 319	pistachio green - vy dk
✳	DMC 701	christmas green - lt
▣	DMC 728	golden yellow
⅄	DMC Ecru	ecru

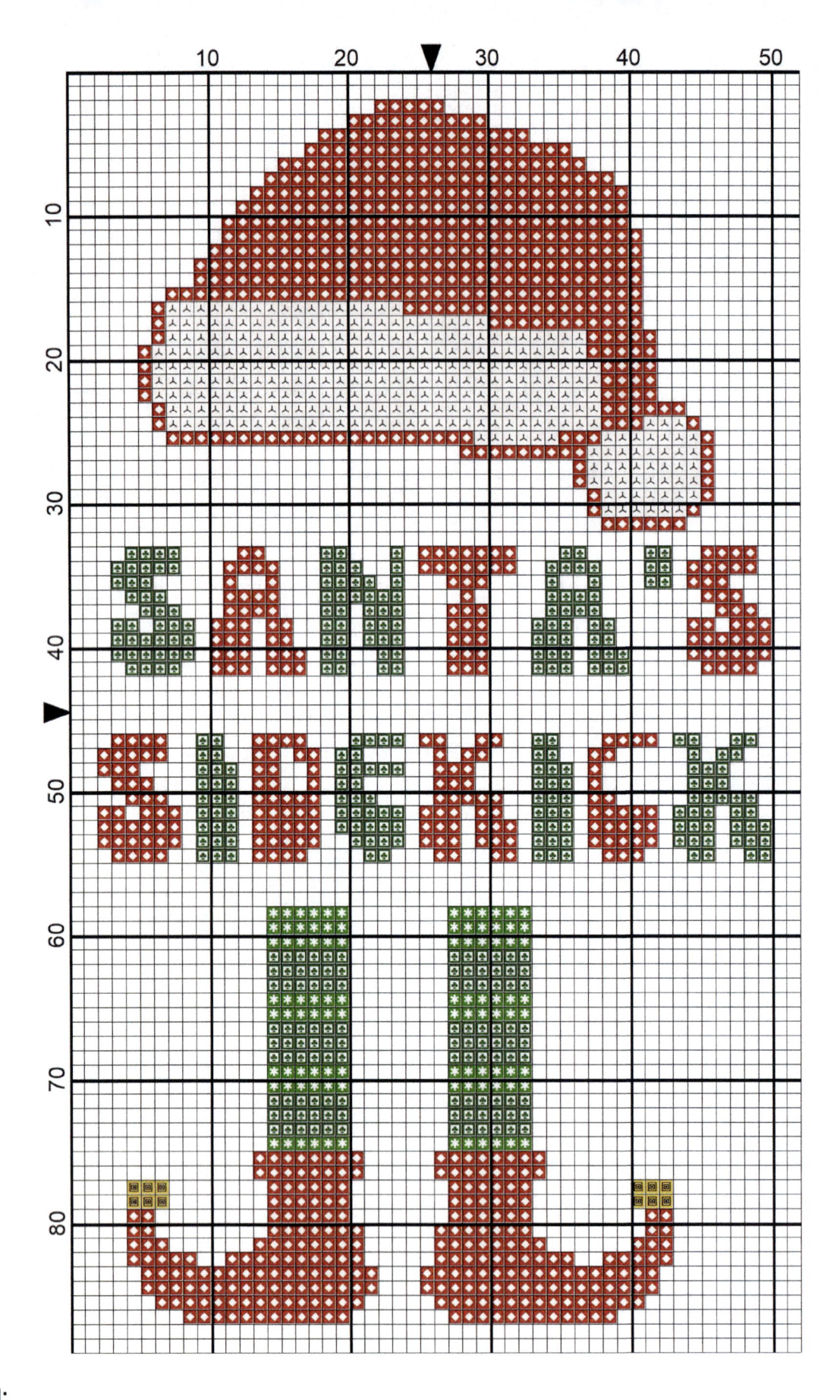

Legend:

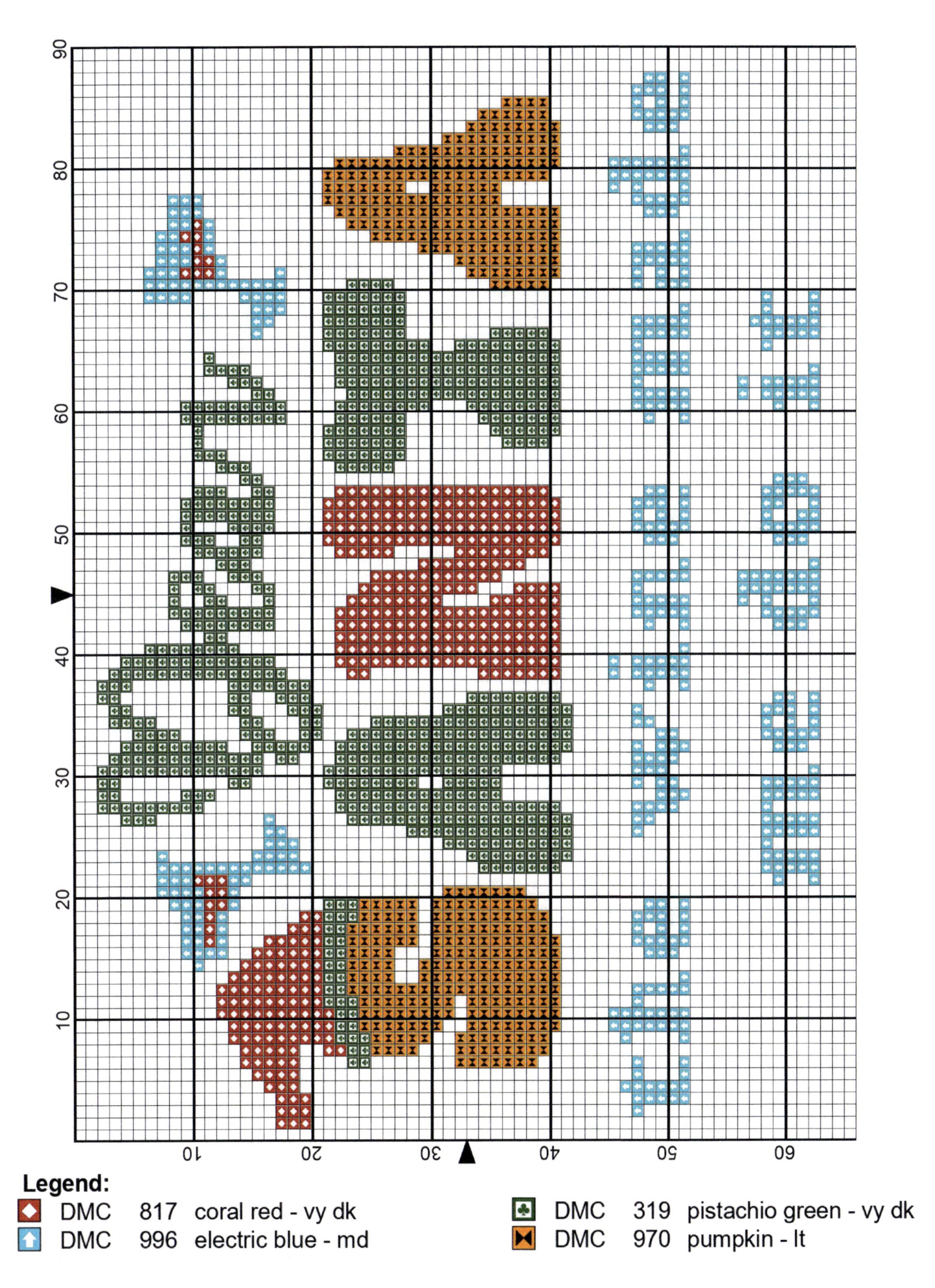

- ◊ DMC 817 coral red - vy dk
- ⬆ DMC 996 electric blue - md
- ♣ DMC 319 pistachio green - vy dk
- ⊠ DMC 970 pumpkin - lt

Legend:

	DMC	817	coral red - vy dk
h	DMC	3841	pale baby blue
	DMC	319	pistachio green - vy dk
	DMC	400	mahogany - dk
	DMC	169	pewter - lt
	DMC	310	black

Legend:

◆ DMC 817 coral red - vy dk   ♣ DMC 319 pistachio green - vy dk

73

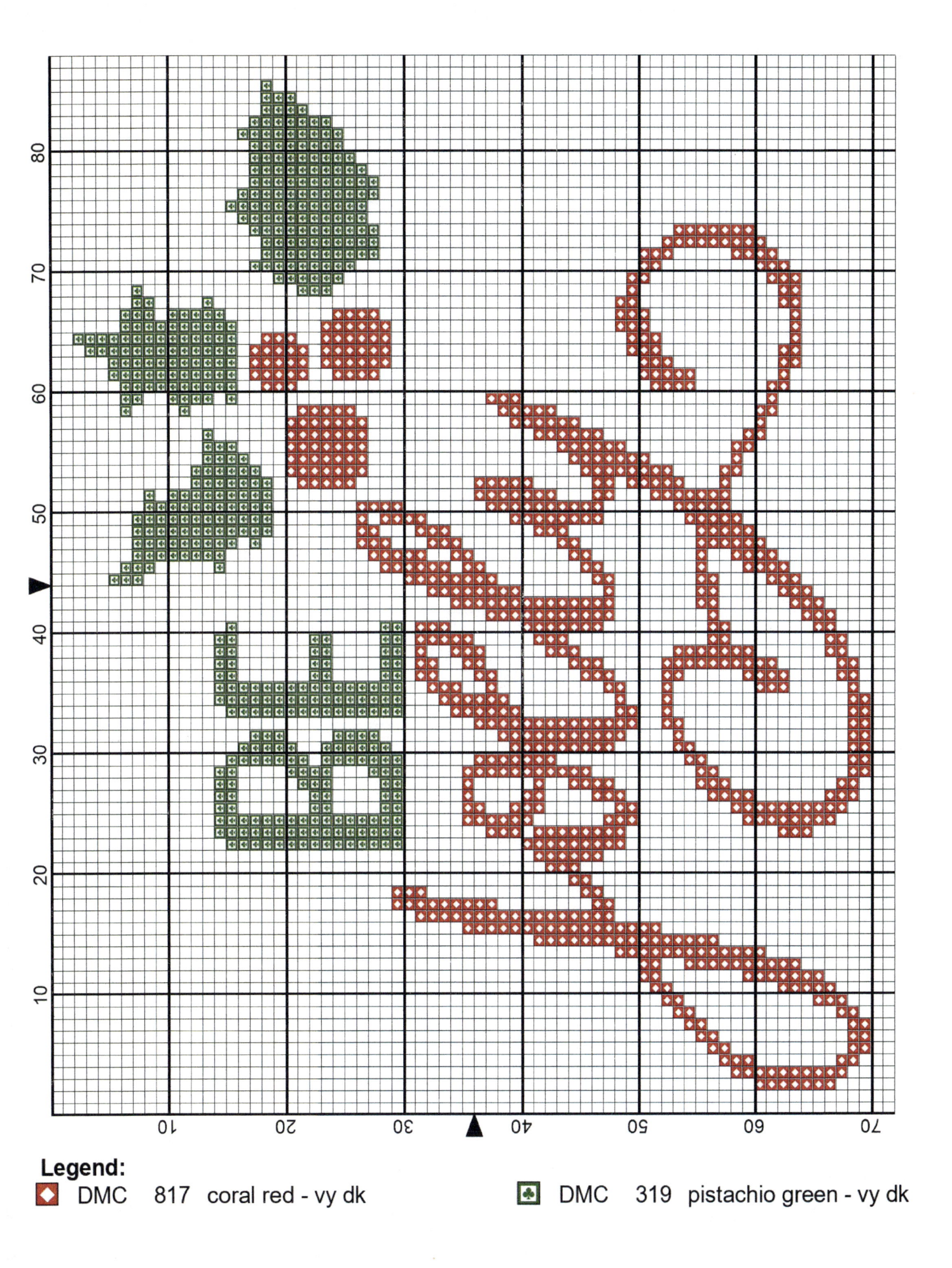

Legend:

◇ DMC 817 coral red - vy dk   ♣ DMC 319 pistachio green - vy dk

Legend:

◆ DMC 817 coral red - vy dk   ♣ DMC 319 pistachio green - vy dk

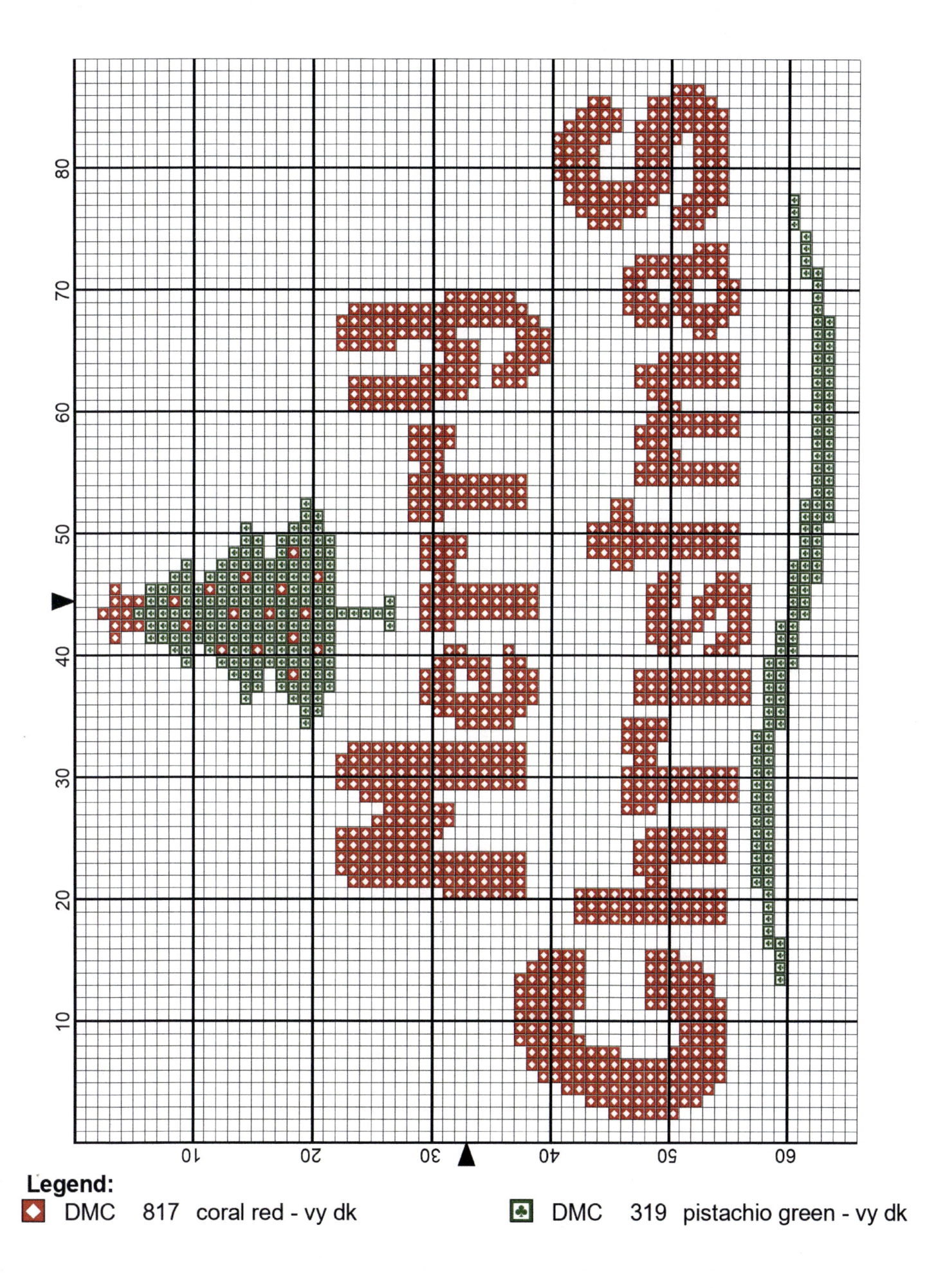

Legend:
- DMC 817 coral red - vy dk
- DMC 319 pistachio green - vy dk
- DMC 728 golden yellow
- DMC 738 tan - vy lt
- DMC 310 black

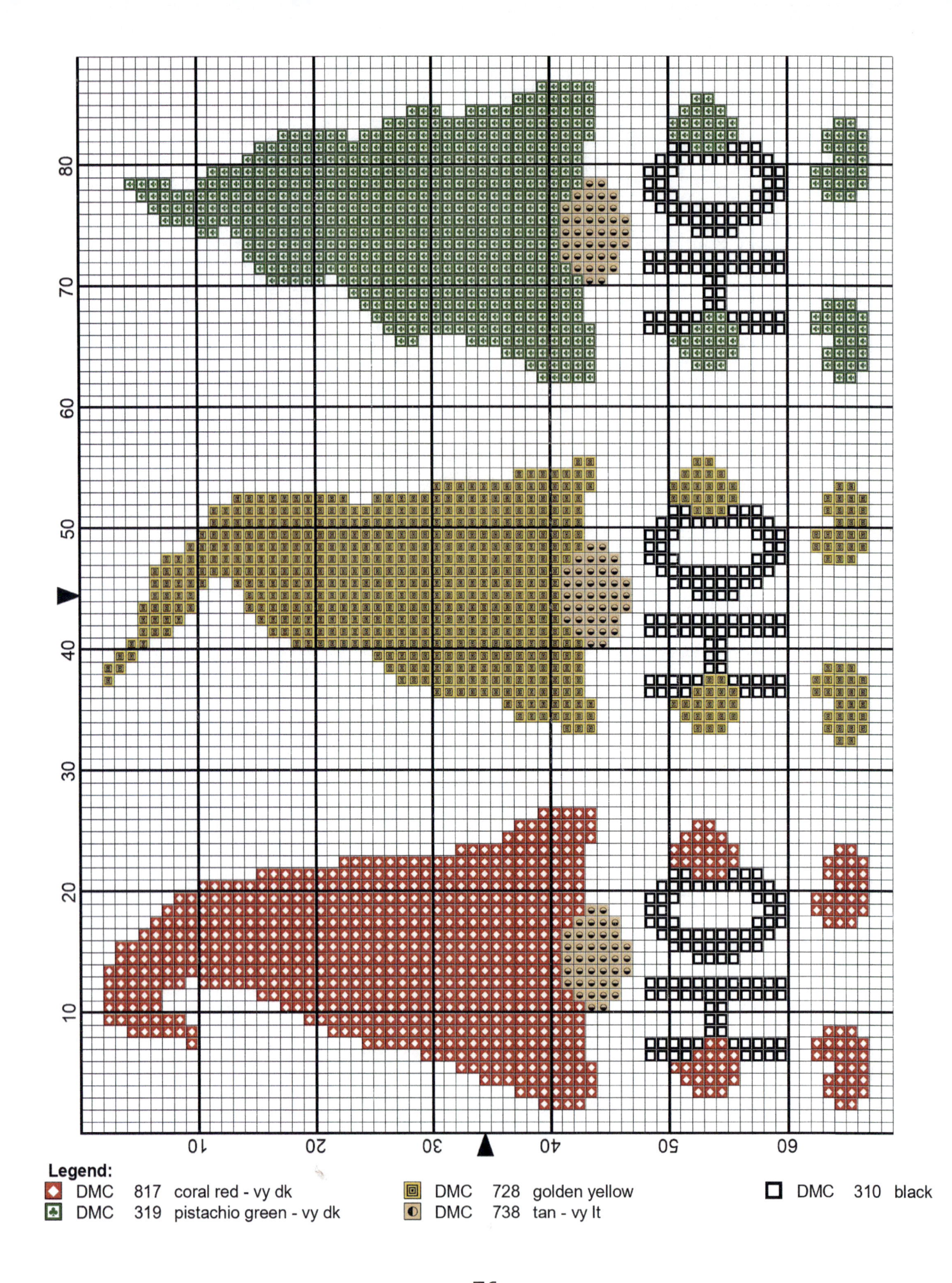

Printed in Dunstable, United Kingdom